Oxford Maths Zone

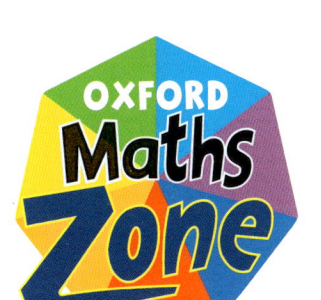

YEAR 4

Core Book

OXFORD
UNIVERSITY PRESS

Oxford Maths Zone is the outcome of a large team effort from many contributors, with a wide range of backgrounds from practising classroom teachers to teacher trainers and Consultants in the National Numeracy Strategy. The project director is Stephen Ashton, and the team of contributors for the Year 4 materials is:

Paul Briten
Bill Bairstow
Barbara Locke
Alison Meechan

Margaret McDougall
Jeanette Mumford
Mary Ruddle

OXFORD
UNIVERSITY PRESS

Great Clarendon Street, Oxford OX2 6DP

Oxford University Press is a department of the University of Oxford.
It furthers the University's objective of excellence in research, scholarship,
and education by publishing worldwide in

Oxford New York

Athens Auckland Bangkok Bogotá Buenos Aires Calcutta
Cape Town Chennai Dar es Salaam Delhi Florence Hong Kong Istanbul
Karachi Kuala Lumpur Madrid Melbourne Mexico City Mumbai
Nairobi Paris São Paulo Singapore Shanghai Taipei Tokyo Toronto Warsaw
with associated companies in Berlin Ibadan

Oxford is a registered trade mark of Oxford University Press
in the UK and in certain other countries

© Oxford University Press 2001

The moral rights of the author have been asserted
Database right Oxford University Press (maker)

First published 2001

All rights reserved. No part of this publication may be reproduced,
stored in a retrieval system, or transmitted, in any form or by any means,
without the prior permission in writing of Oxford University Press,
or as expressly permitted by law, or under terms agreed with the appropriate
reprographics rights organisation. Enquiries concerning reproduction
outside the scope of the above should be sent to the Rights Department,
Oxford University Press, at the address above

You must not circulate this book in any other binding or cover
and you must impose this same condition on any acquirer

British Library Cataloguing in Publication Data

Data available

ISBN 0 19 836068 1

Designed by Oxford Designers and Illustrators
Typeset by Hardlines, Charlbury, Oxford
Printed in Spain by Graficas Estella

Contents

title	page
Term 1	
Travel estimates	5
Addition and subtraction puzzles	6
What can you buy?	7
Different ways to subtract (1)	8
Different ways to subtract (2)	9
Flight savers	10
Measuring in millimetres	11
Recording lengths	12
Measuring problems	13
Perimeters	14
Perimeters of regular polygons	15
Triangle sort	16
Where is it?	17
Review: numbers and problems	18
Review: shapes and measures	19
Odd and even puzzles	20
Puzzle page	21
Dividing	22
Written multiplication	23
Written division	24
Choose operations and methods	25
Fractions of shapes	26
Fractions of quantities	27
Time problems	28
Adding several numbers	29
Three ways to write subtraction	30
Frequency tables	31
Pictograms	32
Interpreting data	33
Review: addition and subtraction	34
Review: choosing the best method	35
Term 2	
Symbols <,>	37
Adding multiples of 10	38
Partitioning	39
Word problems	40
Solving problems	41
Measuring angles	42
Compass directions	43
Shapes and nets	44
Area	45
Estimating mass	46
Kilograms	47
Review: ordering and rounding	48
Review: word problems	49
Number steps	50

title	page
Number sequences	51
Multiplying by 9 and 11	52
Theme Park food problems	53
Dividing pounds	54
Theme Park ride problems	55
Matching fractions	56
Paying for pizza	57
Using decimals	58
Using bar charts (1)	59
Using bar charts (2)	60
Using bar charts (3)	61
Review: multiplication and division facts	62
Review: equivalent fractions	63
Term 3	
Multiplying by 10 and 100	65
Mental addition	66
Mental subtraction	67
Money problems	68
Poster problems	69
Reading scales	70
Capacity maze	71
Capacity problems	72
Reflections	73
Angles	74
Angles on a clock face	75
Regular shapes	76
Exploring shapes	77
Review: tens, hundreds and thousands	78
Review: choosing methods	79
Solving a puzzle	80
Solving number problems	81
Multiplying TU by U	82
Division with remainders	83
Related facts	84
Solving problems and checking results	85
Proportion problems	86
Decimals and fractions	87
Relationship between + and −	88
Add and subtract mentally	89
Addition and subtraction	90
Carroll diagrams	91
Venn diagrams	92
Interpreting data in diagrams	93
Review: multiplication and division	94
Review: addition and subtraction	95
Glossary	96

Term 1

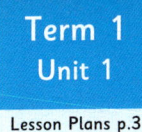

Travel estimates

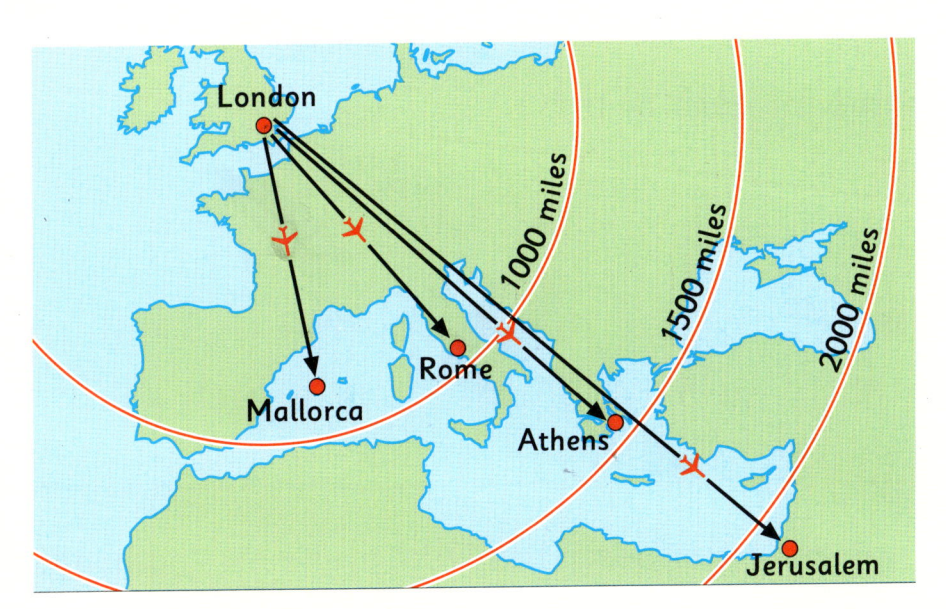

Term 1 Unit 1
Lesson Plans p.3
Q1

1 Estimate how far it is by air from London to:

☆ Mallorca   ☆ about 800 miles

a Rome   **b** Athens   **c** Jerusalem

2 Planes fly 1000 miles in about 2 hours.

Estimate how long it takes to fly to:

☆ Mallorca   ☆ about 2 hours

a Rome   **b** Athens   **c** Jerusalem

Challenge

3 Look at the aeroplanes on the map.

Estimate the distance they have travelled and how much further they have left to go. How much journey time is left?

Addition and subtraction puzzles

1 Write four sums for each of these:

☆ 20 + 8 = ■

> 20 + 8 = 28
> 8 + 20 = 28
> 28 − 8 = 20
> 28 − 20 = 8 ✓

a 19 + 9 = ■
b 20 + 15 = ■
c 25 + 26 = ■
d 53 + 19 = ■
e 49 + 48 = ■
f 35 + 65 = ■

2 Copy these number pyramids. Then write in the missing numbers.

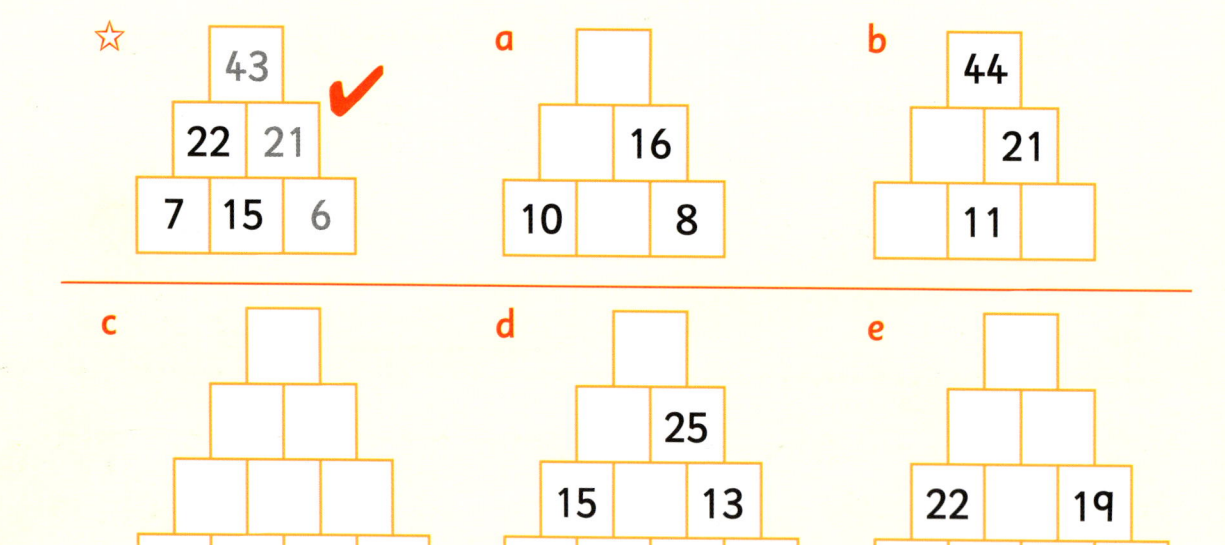

☆
```
      43 ✓
   22   21
  7  15   6
```

a
```
         
      16
   10    8
```

b
```
      44
         21
         11
```

c
```
         
         
         
  5  4  3  6
```

d
```
      
      25
   15    13
      7    8
```

e
```
      
         
   22    19
   11    10
```

Challenge

3 Draw a four-layer number pyramid. Write in four numbers. Is there more than one solution? Can you place the numbers so there is only one solution? Where did you put the numbers?

Where shall I put them?

What can you buy?

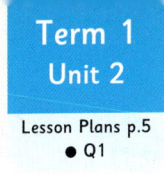

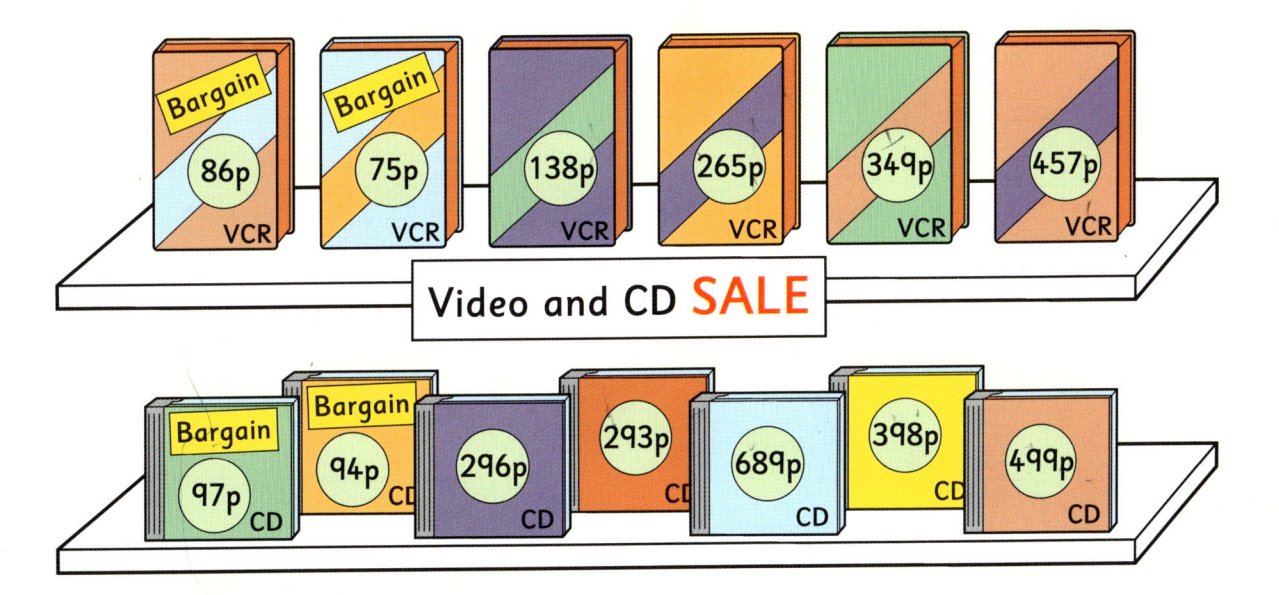

Term 1 Unit 2
Lesson Plans p.5
● Q1

VCR prices: 86p, 75p, 138p, 265p, 349p, 457p

Video and CD **SALE**

CD prices: 97p, 94p, 296p, 293p, 689p, 398p, 499p

1 You have £2 to spend on videos and CDs.

Make three more different addition calculations.

> 100
> 86 + 97 = 186
> 186 − 3 = 183
>
> I rounded to 100 then took off the 3

2 You buy a video and a CD in the sale – but not 'yellow sticker' bargains.

Write six different addition calculations.

> 400
> 138 + 398 = 538
> 538 − 2 = 536
>
> I rounded to 400 then took off the 2

Challenge

3 You have £10 to spend on CDs.

Excluding the 'yellow sticker' CDs, which three CDs can you buy?

7

Different ways to subtract (1)

Term 1 Unit 3 — Lesson Plans p.6 • Q1

1 Copy each number line.

Use it to show the subtraction.

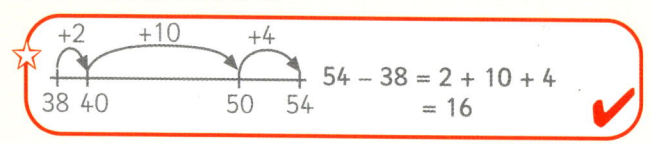

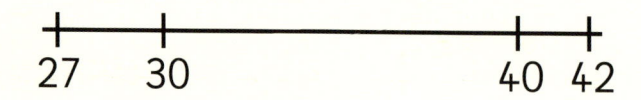

☆ 54 − 38

+2 +10 +4
38 40   50 54
54 − 38 = 2 + 10 + 4 = 16 ✓

a 42 − 27

27 30   40 42

b 76 − 54

54   76

c 92 − 43

43   92

2 Do these subtractions. Show them in two different ways.

☆ 137 − 82

+8 +10 +37
82 90 100   137
8 + 10 + 37 = 55 ✓

```
        137
    −    82
82 → 90    8
90 → 100  10
100 → 137 37
137 − 82 = 55  ✓
```

a 164 − 76

b 153 − 91

c 250 − 172

d 513 − 250

e 3000 − 2884

f 4006 − 3950

Challenge

3 Use your own method to find the missing number.

Which is the odd one out?

a 550 − ■ = 427

b 760 − ■ = 427

c 1883 − ■ = 1427

Different ways to subtract (2)

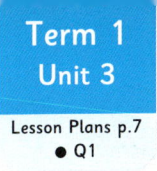

Term 1 Unit 3
Lesson Plans p.7
• Q1

1 Copy each number line.
Use it to show the subtraction.

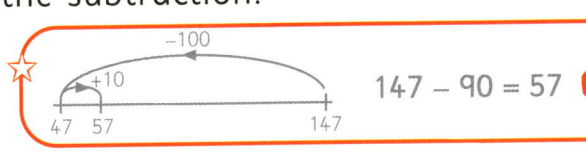

think to the nearest 100

☆ 147 − 90

$$147 - 90 = 57 \checkmark$$

a 165 − 91

b 176 − 94

c 138 − 95

2 Do these subtractions. Show your working. ☆ 236 − 88

a 365 − 91
b 430 − 185
c 527 − 294
d 407 − 196
e 553 − 392
f 727 − 484

```
      236
    −  88
(−100) → 136
(+12)  → + 12
236 − 88 = 148 ✓
```

Challenge

3 **Go clockwise.** Copy each puzzle.

When the next number is larger, write the difference **outside** the line.

When it is smaller, write it inside.

Total inside numbers, then outside numbers. What happens?

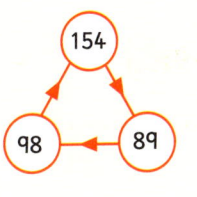

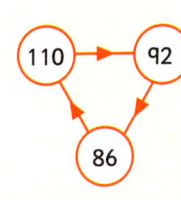

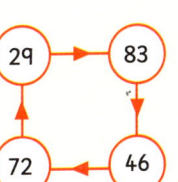

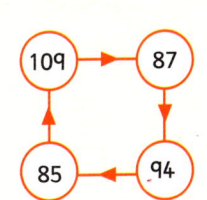

Flight savers

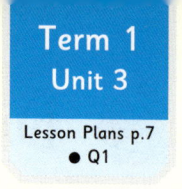

dontmissit.com
Cheap flights!
New York £177
Cairo £285
Sydney £550
Bangkok £375

ohnozone.com
Where do you want to go?
Sydney £435
Bangkok £299
Cairo £227
New York £225

1 How much do you save if you go the cheaper way?

☆ New York £225 − £177 = £48 ✓

a Sydney **b** Bangkok **c** Cairo

2 Fly to two cities. You must use the same airline each time. How much can you save now?

☆ New York and Cairo £177 + £285 = £462
  £225 + £227 = £452
  £462 − £452 = £10 ✓

a New York and Bangkok
b Cairo and Sydney
c Bangkok and Cairo
d New York and Sydney

Challenge

3 Look at this puzzle from an in-flight magazine.

What numbers go in boxes a, b, c, d and e?

320	+	239	=	a
+	■	+	■	+
b	+	d	=	417
=	■	=	■	=
c	+	480	=	e

Measuring in millimetres

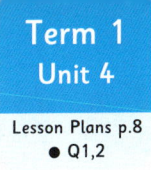

1 Draw lines of these lengths:

☆ 30 mm

a 75 mm

b 45 mm

c 70 mm

d 55 mm

e 90 mm

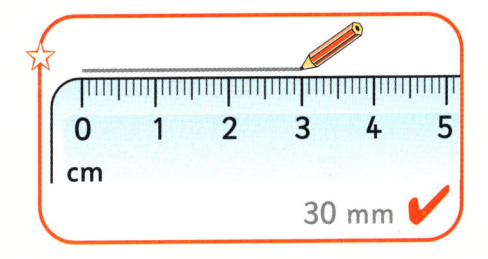

30 mm ✓

2 Measure the pencils in millimetres.
Record the lengths in two ways.

☆ 60 mm
6 cm 0 mm ✓

a
b
c
d
e

3 Draw a line:

a 20 mm longer than 85 mm.

b twice as long as 45 mm.

c 4 cm shorter than 65 mm.

d half as long as 130 mm.

Challenge

4 Estimate, then measure in millimetres, the distance between the points of any six pairs of pencils in Question 2.

Recording lengths

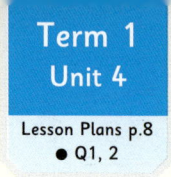

Term 1 Unit 4
Lesson Plans p.8
● Q1, 2

The drawings show parts of measuring tapes.
Read the measurements at each arrow.
Record in centimetres and then in metres.

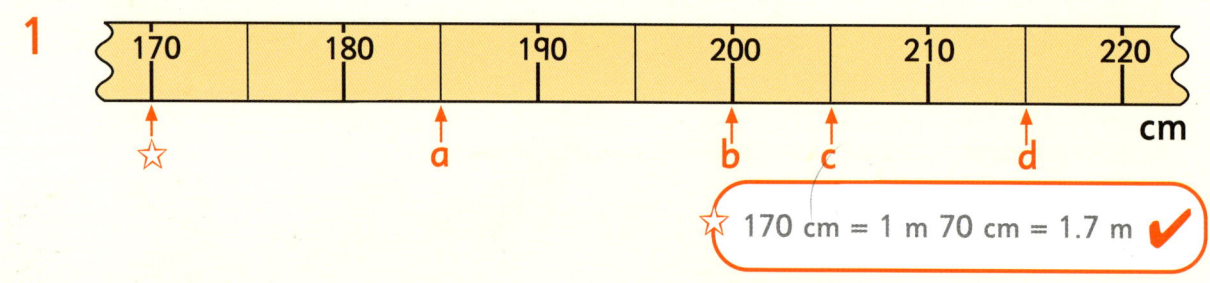

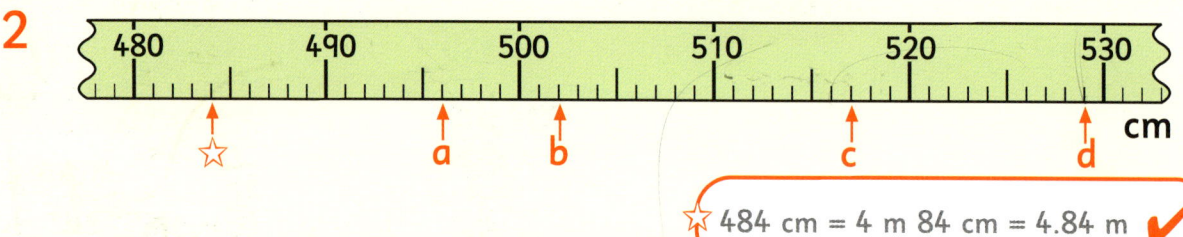

1 [tape showing 170, 180, 190, 200, 210, 220 cm with arrows ☆, a, b, c, d]

☆ 170 cm = 1 m 70 cm = 1.7 m ✓

2 [tape showing 480, 490, 500, 510, 520, 530 cm with arrows ☆, a, b, c, d]

☆ 484 cm = 4 m 84 cm = 4.84 m ✓

3 Copy and complete.

a 6.16 m = ■ cm

b 5.68 m = ■ cm

c 5.38 m = ■ cm

☆ 7.42 m = 742 cm ✓

d 8.76 m = ■ cm

e 4.05 m = ■ cm

Challenge

4 You have four strips of wood.

What different lengths can you make by fitting any two strips together?

What if . . .
you fitted three strips together?

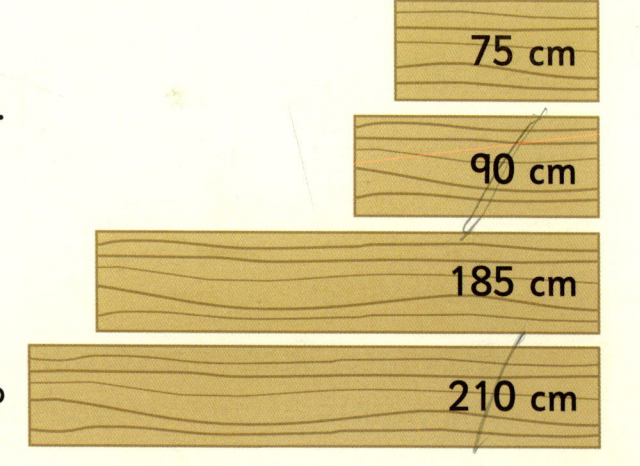

75 cm
90 cm
185 cm
210 cm

Measurement problems

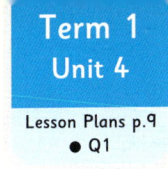

Term 1 Unit 4
Lesson Plans p.9
• Q1

1 Each 10 m bus is parked $\frac{1}{4}$ m from the bus in front.

How long, from end to end, is a line of five buses?

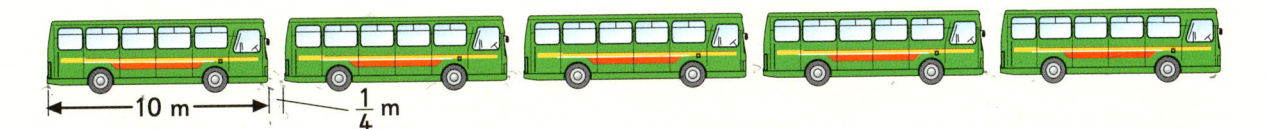

2 Jim's cousin is 96 cm tall.

The piper is twice his height.

How tall is the piper?

depth: 1m 20 cm

depth: 3 m

3 How much deeper is the water at the deep end than the shallow end?

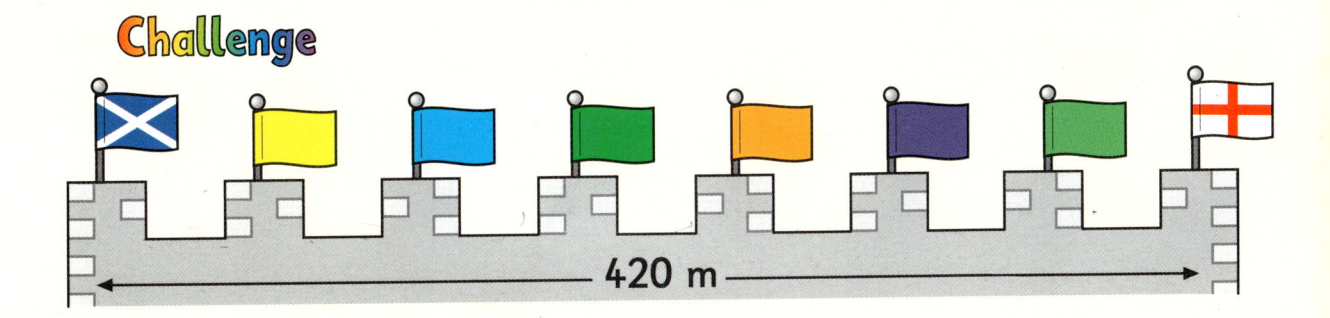

Challenge

420 m

4 There is a flagpole at each end of the Castle Esplanade and six flagpoles in between. The Esplanade is 420 m long.

What is the distance between each flagpole?

Perimeters

Term 1 Unit 5
Lesson Plans p.10
● Q1

1 Work out the perimeter of each shape.

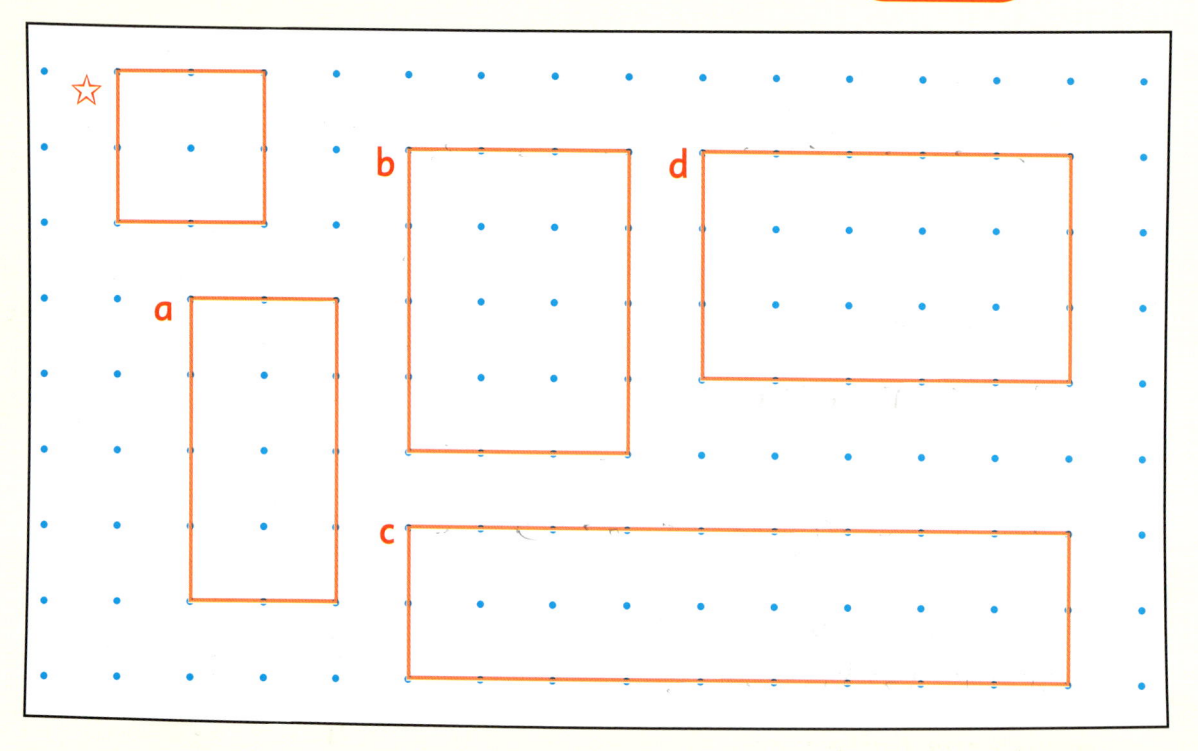

☆ 8 cm ✓

2 a Draw two different sized squares on 1 cm dotty paper.
  b Find the perimeter of each square.

Challenge

3 a Draw this shape on dotty paper and work out its perimeter.

  b Draw more six-square shapes. What are their perimeters?

  c What do you notice?

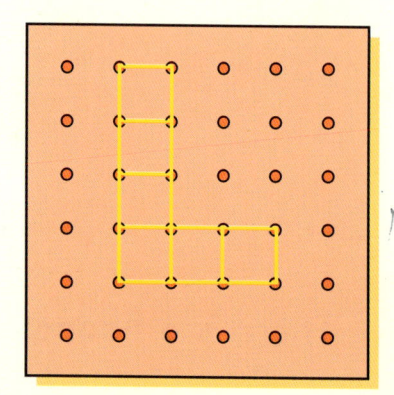

Perimeters of regular polygons

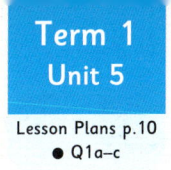

1 Look at this sequence of joined squares:

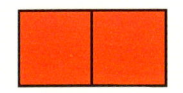

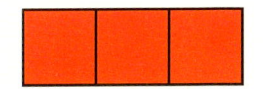

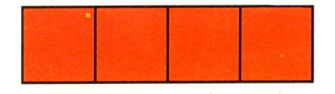

a Copy and complete the table up to four squares.

b Predict the perimeter for:
5 squares
6 squares

c Look for a pattern. Write, in words, how the pattern works.

d Use the pattern to complete the table.

number of squares	perimeter in centimetres
1	
2	☆ 6
3	
4	
5	
6	
7	
8	
9	
10	

Challenge

2 These hexagons have 1 cm sides.

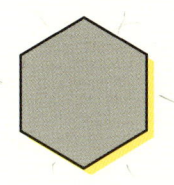

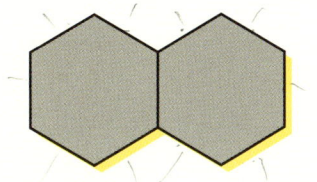

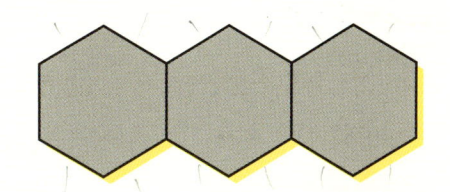

Find a way to work out the perimeter of a hexagon pattern that is five hexagons long.

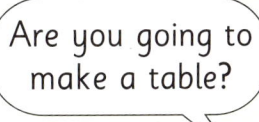

Are you going to make a table?

Triangle sort

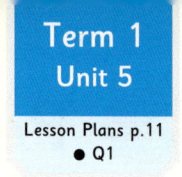

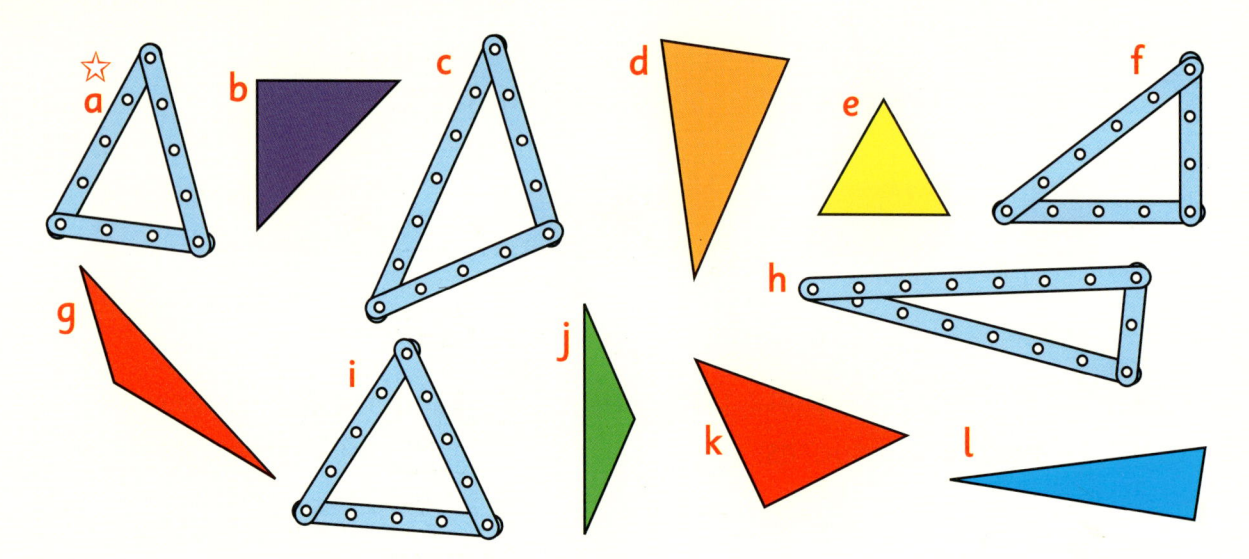

1 Copy this table into your book.

Sort the triangles.

equilateral	isosceles	other
	☆ a	

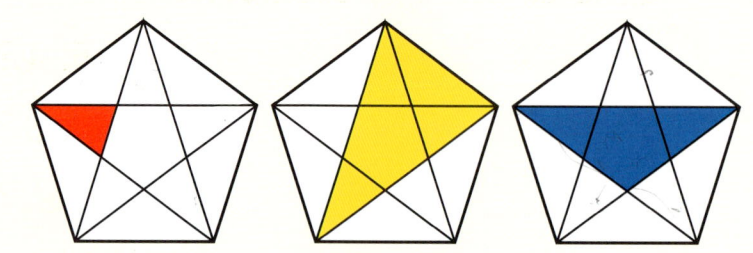

Challenge

2 You can find different isosceles triangles in a pentagon.

How many isosceles triangles are the same as:

a the red triangle?

b the yellow triangle?

c the blue triangle?

Where is it?

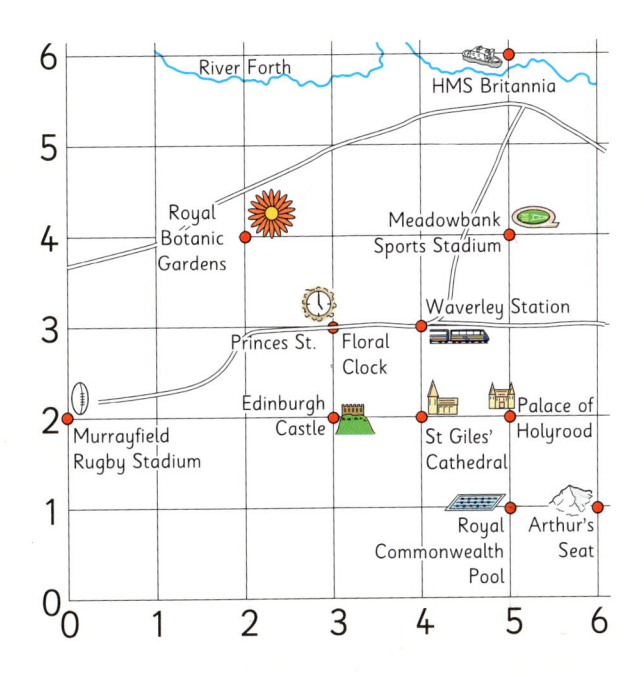

1 Write the co-ordinates for:

☆ Edinburgh Castle ☆ (3, 2)
a St Giles' Cathedral
b Murrayfield Rugby Stadium
c Waverley Station
d Royal Botanic Gardens
e Palace of Holyrood

2 What is at these co-ordinates:

a (5, 1)?
b (6, 1)?
c (2, 4)?
d (5, 4)?
e (3, 3)?
f (5, 6)?

Challenge

3 a Find three places which have a second co-ordinate of 2.

b Find three places which have co-ordinates totalling 6.

c Make up another co-ordinate puzzle.

Review: numbers and problems

1 Copy and complete the table:

Number	Value of digits
☆ 5634	5000 + 600 + 30 + 4 ✓
3918	
8693	
2268	
1830	

2 Max went aeroplanespotting at the airport.

He counted the number of aeroplanes which landed and the number which took off each hour. The chart shows how many he saw.

Time	Landings	Take offs
hour 1	93	62
hour 2	147	76
hour 3	109	168

☆ How many landings and take offs did he see in hour 1?

☆ 93 + 62 = 100 + 62 – 7
= 162 – 7
= 155
He saw 155 in hour 1.

a How many landings and take offs did he see in hour 2?

b How many more aeroplanes took off in hour 3 than in hour 1?

c How many more aeroplanes took off in hour 3 than in hour 2?

d How many aeroplanes took off altogether?

e Altogether, how many more aeroplanes landed than took off?

Review: shapes and measures

Term 1 Unit 7
Lesson Plans p.13

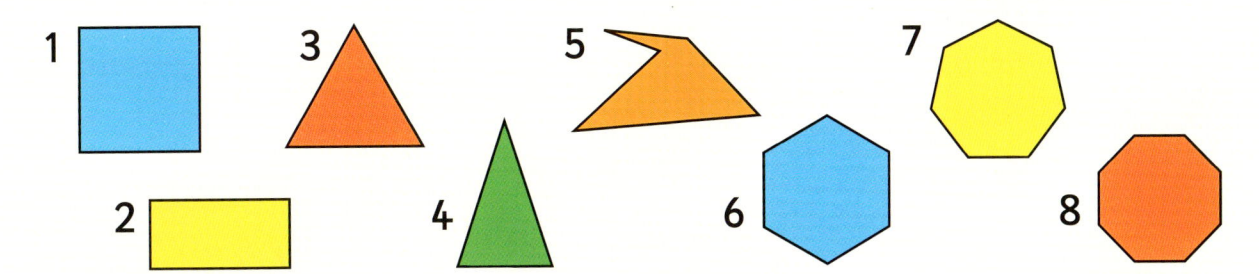

1 Write the number of each shape which:

☆ has 4 sides — 1, 2 ✓

a is regular

b has right angles

c is an isosceles triangle

d is a heptagon

e is symmetrical

2 Write these lengths in order. ☆ $\frac{1}{10}$ km,

Start with the shortest.

a 500 m $1\frac{1}{2}$ km   ☆ $\frac{1}{10}$ km $\frac{3}{4}$ km   200 m

b 75 cm $\frac{1}{4}$ m   20 cm $\frac{9}{10}$ m $\frac{1}{2}$ m

3 What is the difference in wingspan between:

☆ 95 − 25 = 70
The difference is 70 cm. ✓

☆ a thrush and a duck?

a a thrush and an eagle?

b a duck and an albatross?

c an eagle and an albatross?

d a thrush and an albatross?

bird	wingspan
thrush	25 cm
duck	95 cm
eagle	220 cm
albatross	315 cm

Odd and even puzzles

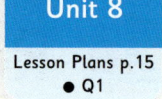

Term 1 Unit 8
Lesson Plans p.15 • Q1

1 Choose pairs of numbers to add. Make even-number answers.

☆ 13   24   7   ☆ 9 + 13 = 22 ✓

☆ 9   35   26   46

12   17   21

2 Write the next three numbers. What is the rule?

☆ 26, 33, 40, ■, ■, ■

a 57, 48, 39, ■, ■, ■

b 635, 535, 435, ■, ■, ■

c 103, 111, 119, ■, ■, ■

d 108, 106, 104, ■, ■, ■

e 173, 183, 193, ■, ■, ■

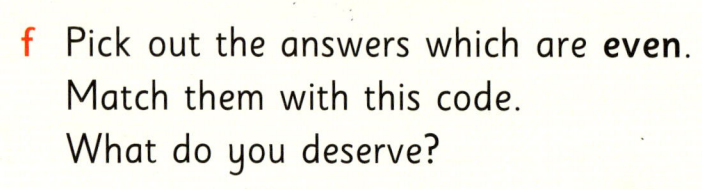

☆ 47, 54, 61
Count on 7 each time ✓

f Pick out the answers which are **even**.
Match them with this code.
What do you deserve?

54, that's even 54 = R

12 = W   30 = E   54 = R   98 = D   100 = R   102 = A

Challenge

3 a Draw three boxes.

b Use the six odd numbers from 9 to 19, once each.

Write two numbers in each box but...

RULE each box must have the same total.

20

Puzzle page

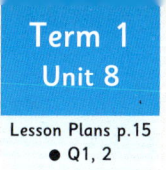

1 Copy the puzzle.

Put 1, 2, 3, 4, 5, 6, 7 or 9 in each box but...

RULE each side totals 12

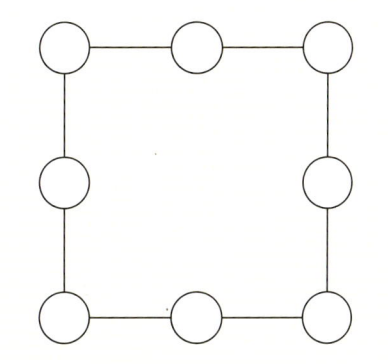

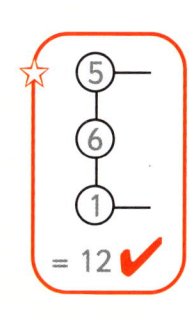

☆ 5 — 6 — 1 = 12 ✔

---

2 Find a pair of numbers with:

	a sum of	a product of
☆	13	30
a	10	16
b	7	12

☆ 3, 10 ✔

---

3 Find three consecutive numbers which add up to make:

☆ 18   ☆ 5, 6, 7 ✔

a 12

b 27

Challenge

4 Copy the triangle puzzle.

Put 1, 2, and 3 in the spaces but...

RULE each side must have the same total.

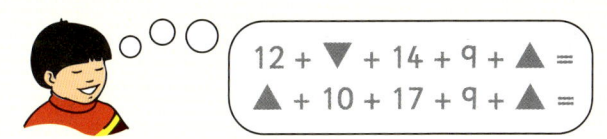

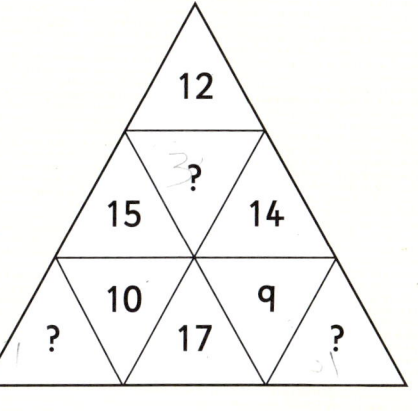

$12 + \blacktriangledown + 14 + 9 + \blacktriangle =$
$\blacktriangle + 10 + 17 + 9 + \blacktriangle =$

Triangle values: 12, ?, 15, 14, 10, 9, ?, 17, ?

Make a triangle puzzle for your partner.

21

Dividing

Term 1 Unit 9
Lesson Plans p.16
● Q1–3

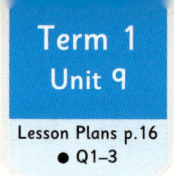

$36 \div 4 = 9$

1 Share 36 between:

☆ 4   a 3   b 6   c 2

☆ $36 \div 4 = 9$ ✓

I know $9 \times 4 = 36$ so $36 \div 4 = 9$

2 Divide:

a 40 by 5   b 63 by 3   c 24 by 2   d 28 by 4

3 How many groups of 5 can be made from:

a 20?   b 15?   c 45?   d 35?   e 60?

4 Write the sum with its answer in your exercise book.

a $80 \div 8 = \triangle$
b $24 \div \triangle = 3$
c $\triangle \div 10 = 7$
d $\triangle \div 7 = 5$
e $18 \div 2 = \triangle$
f $45 \div \triangle = 9$

Challenge

5 Draw machines to show:

a $12 \div 3$ b 4×3

Written multiplication

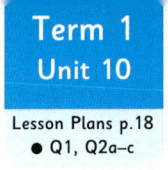

Term 1 Unit 10
Lesson Plans p.18
● Q1, Q2a–c

1 Work out an approximate answer to:

☆ 43 × 9   ☆ 43 × 9 is approximately 40 × 10 = 400 ✓

a 33 × 8   d 84 × 9   g 64 × 9
b 19 × 9   e 22 × 8   h 44 × 8
c 52 × 9   f 73 × 9

Choose from these answers:

100   200   300   ☆400   500   600   700   800

Which questions have approximately the same answer?

2 Approximate first, then draw grids to find the exact answer.

☆ 23 × 8

☆ 20 × 10 = 200 ✓
| × | 20 | 3 |
| 8 | 160 | 24 | = 184 ✓

a 62 × 9   c 34 × 9   e 51 × 9
b 23 × 7   d 74 × 9   f 43 × 9

Challenge

3 a Write five multiplication questions with an approximate answer of 200.

 b Find the actual answer to each question. Use a calculator to help if you wish.

 c Ring the answer that came closest to 200.

23

Written division

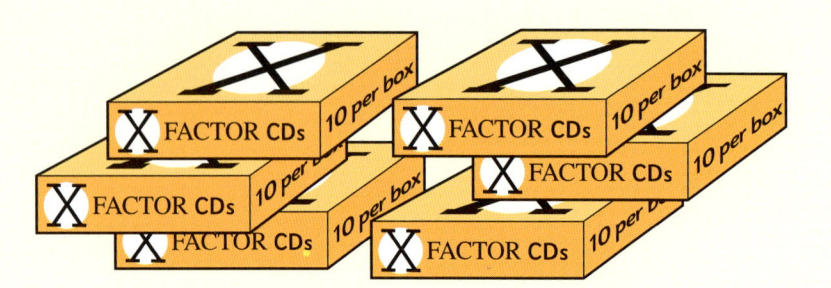

Term 1
Unit 10
Lesson Plans p.18
• Q1a–d, Q2a–c

How many boxes for 60 CDs?

$60 \div 10 = 6$

1 Find the answer by dividing.
Show your workings.

☆ $60 \div 5 = \blacksquare$

a $84 \div 4 = \blacksquare$
b $65 \div 5 = \blacksquare$
c $72 \div 4 = \blacksquare$
d $92 \div 4 = \blacksquare$
e $87 \div 3 = \blacksquare$
f $56 \div 4 = \blacksquare$

☆
```
    60
  - 50    10 × 5
  ----
    10
  - 10    2 × 5
  ----
     0
```
Answer: 12 ✓

2 Choose your own method of working.
Record how you worked out the answer.

☆ $41 \div 4 = \blacksquare$

a $32 \div 3 = \blacksquare$
b $46 \div 4 = \blacksquare$
c $79 \div 5 = \blacksquare$
d $28 \div 3 = \blacksquare$
e $57 \div 4 = \blacksquare$
f $97 \div 5 = \blacksquare$

☆ I know $4 \times 10 = 40$
so $41 \div 4 = 10\ r1$ ✓

Challenge

3 Find the two mystery numbers.

Their quotient is 12.
Their product is 48.

Make up a mystery puzzle for your partner.

Choose operations and methods

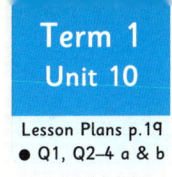

Term 1 Unit 10
Lesson Plans p.19
● Q1, Q2–4 a & b

Record your workings using numbers, signs and symbols.

1. **Programmes cost £12 each.** Find the cost of:

   ☆ three programmes

   a 10 programmes

   b 50 programmes

   c 16 programmes

   > ☆ Three programmes at £12
   > = 3 × £10 + 3 × £2
   > = £36 ✓

2. **Find the cost of:**

   ☆ a T-shirt and a badge

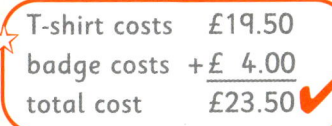

   > ☆ T-shirt costs   £19.50
   >   badge costs   +£ 4.00
   >   total cost   £23.50 ✓

   a two CDs

   b a photograph and a CD

   T-shirt £19.50
   CD £13.25
   badge £4.00
   framed photo £7.70

3. Find the change from £20 when you buy:

   a a T-shirt   b a photograph and a badge   c a badge and a CD

4. How many badges can you buy for:

   a £20   b £84   c £50   d £100

5. You were given £12.30 change from £20. Draw the article you bought.

Challenge

6. **You have £25.**
   List all the items or combinations of items you could buy with that amount.

25

Fractions of shapes

Term 1 Unit 11
Lesson Plans p.20
● Q1 a–e

1 What fraction is:

☆ red? ☆ $\frac{1}{4}$ or one-quarter ✓

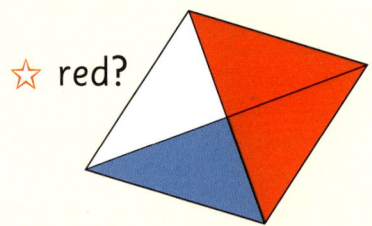

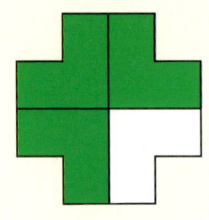

a green?

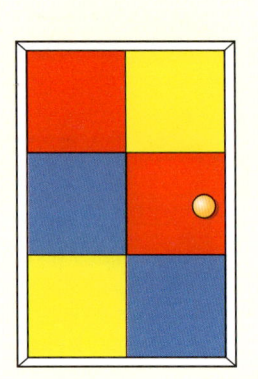

b yellow?

c brown?

d three pieces of chocolate?

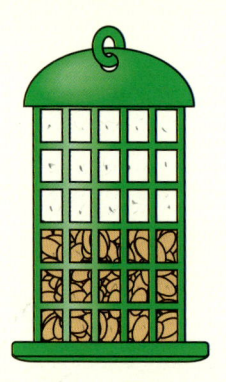

e filled with nuts?

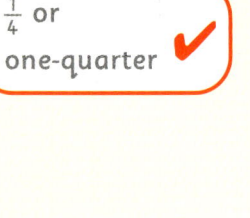

f black?

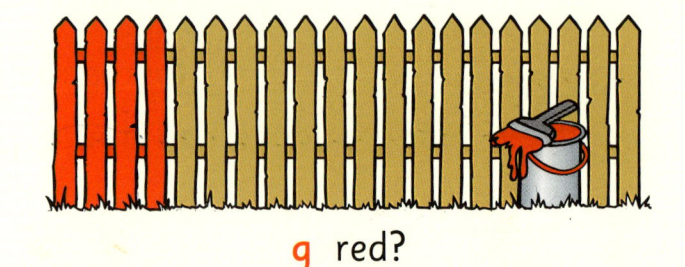

g red?

Challenge

2 Use squared paper.
Cut out shapes of 20 squares and colour them to show: four-fifths; three-tenths; seven-twentieths.

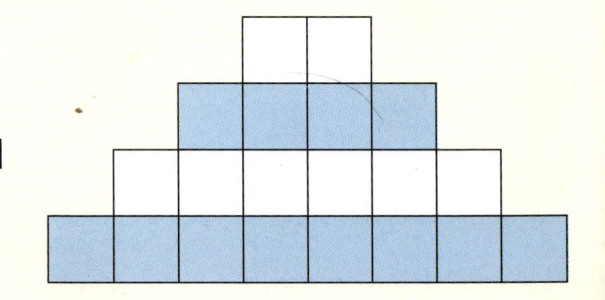

Fractions of quantities

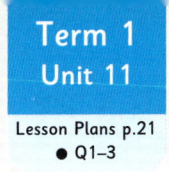

Term 1 Unit 11
Lesson Plans p.21
• Q1–3

1 How many biscuits are in:

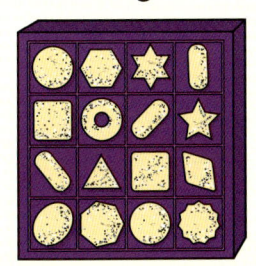

☆ one-half of the tray?

a one-quarter?

b one-eighth?

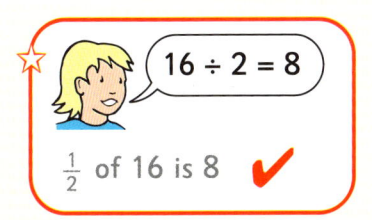

> 16 ÷ 2 = 8
>
> $\frac{1}{2}$ of 16 is 8 ✓

2 How much does each item cost if Steve spends:

a $\frac{1}{2}$ of his money on a comic?

b $\frac{1}{5}$ on a drink?

3 Find:

a one-tenth of	b $\frac{1}{4}$ of	c one-sixth of
40 400	12 40 20	12 60

Match your answers with the code to find the name of a chirpy insect written backwards.

40 = E   3 = K   5 = I   2 = R   10 = C   4 = T

Challenge

4 What fraction of the whole shape is one small triangle?

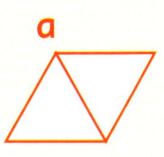

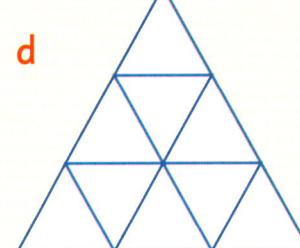

a   b   c   d

e Use triangular lattice paper to draw a shape. What fraction of your whole shape is one triangle? Ask your partner to name the fraction.

27

Time problems

1 Record your answer in words.

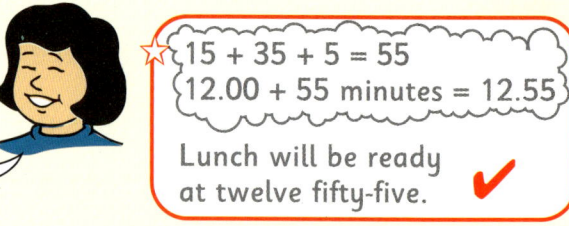

> Mum, it's 12 o'clock. When will lunch be ready?
>
> It will take 15 minutes to prepare, 35 minutes to cook, and 5 minutes to serve.

> ☆ 15 + 35 + 5 = 55
> 12.00 + 55 minutes = 12.55
> Lunch will be ready at twelve fifty-five. ✓

a It takes Rob 17 minutes to walk to school. At what time should he leave home to arrive at 9:00 a.m?

b A train leaves at 12:19 p.m. The journey takes 46 minutes. When should it arrive?

c It took Eva 36 minutes to blow up 18 balloons. How long did she take to blow up one balloon?

d Salma finished making a model ship at 2:15 p.m. It takes $1\frac{1}{2}$ hours for the glue to dry. When will it be dry?

2 Record workings and answers.

☆ You get up at 7:45 a.m. It takes 25 minutes to shower and dress and 20 minutes to eat breakfast. At what time will you leave for school?

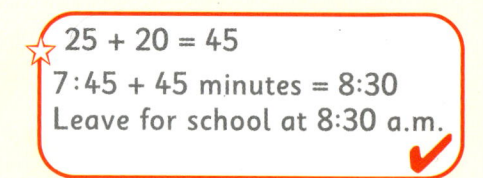

> ☆ 25 + 20 = 45
> 7:45 + 45 minutes = 8:30
> Leave for school at 8:30 a.m. ✓

a The football match started at 1:45 p.m. They played 45 minutes each way, with a 10 minute break. At what time did the game finish?

b You must be on stage at 7:00 p.m. It will take 18 minutes to walk to the hall, 20 minutes to have your make-up done, 25 minutes to put on your costume. At what time do you need to leave home?

Challenge

3 Work out how many hours you sleep in a week. How many in a year?

Adding several numbers

1 Estimate which answer will be closest to **400**.

   a 419 + 37   **b** 365 + 59   **c** 333 + 98

2 Work out the totals accurately.
Line the numbers up in the correct columns.
Choose whether to add the units or the hundreds first.

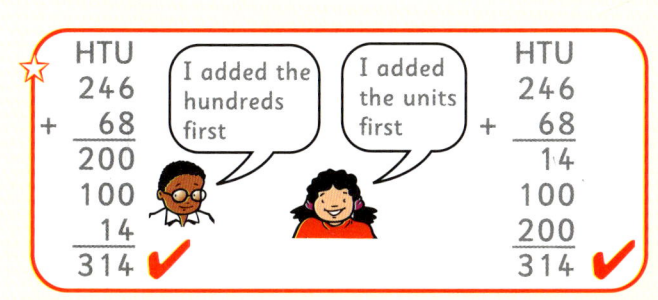

☆ 246 + 68

```
  HTU            HTU
  246            246
+  68          +  68
  200             14
  100            100
   14            200
  314 ✓         314 ✓
```
"I added the hundreds first" "I added the units first"

  a 419 + 37

  b 365 + 59

  c 333 + 98

  d Was your estimate in Question 1 correct?

3 If you do these correctly, the answers should match in pairs.

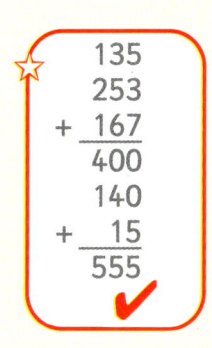

☆ 135 + 253 + 167

```
   135
   253
+  167
   400
   140
+   15
   555 ✓
```

  a 148 + 116 + 447

  b 18 + 666 + 27

  c 359 + 17 + 8

  d 346 + 6 + 118 + 23

  e 54 + 200 + 17 + 113

  f 4 + 225 + 174 + 58 + 32

Challenge

4 Find four numbers which total 500.
One must be a single digit number.
One must be a two-digit number.
One must be a three-digit number.
Ask your partner to check.

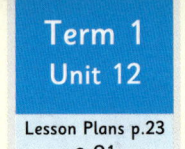

Three ways to write subtraction

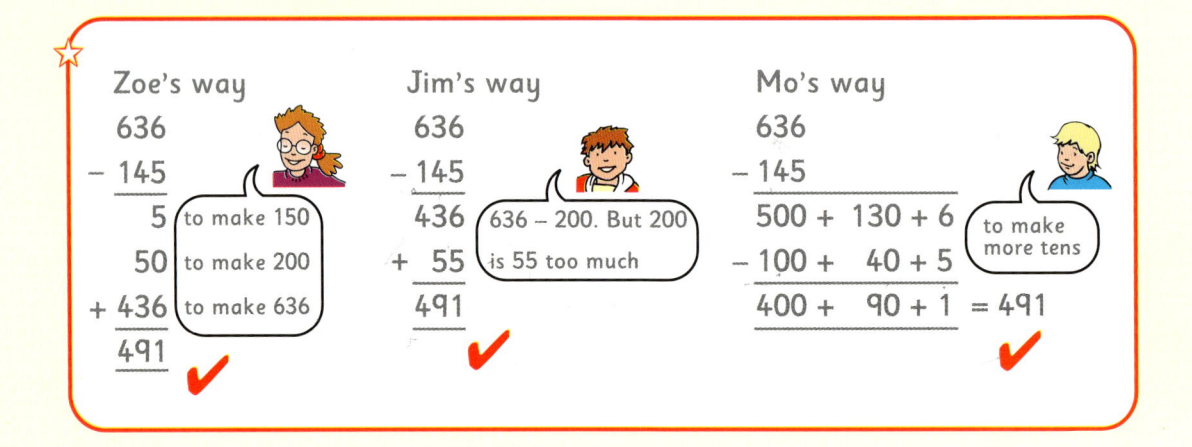

Zoe's way
```
  636
-  145
-----
    5   to make 150
   50   to make 200
+ 436   to make 636
-----
  491  ✓
```

Jim's way
```
  636
-  145
-----
  436   636 – 200. But 200
+  55   is 55 too much
-----
  491  ✓
```

Mo's way
```
  636            500 + 130 + 6     to make
-  145         – 100 +  40 + 5     more tens
-----          ------------------
                 400 +  90 + 1  = 491  ✓
```

1 Do these Mo's way.

    a   457   **b**   726
        – 172   – 243

2 Choose a way to do these.

    a   529   **b**   462   **c**   615   **d**   324
       – 176   – 180   – 263   – 283

Challenge

3 300 young trout were released into a river. How many were left if the herons ate …?

The answer is 127. How many trout did the herons eat? Write another subtraction problem which has the answer 127. Ask your partner to check it.

Term 1
Unit 12
Lesson Plans p.23
● Q1

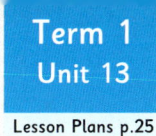

Frequency tables

1 In a survey of water sports, 126 people chose water-skiing, 239 chose sailing, 142 chose surfing and 625 chose swimming.

Draw a frequency table to show this information. Give the table a heading.

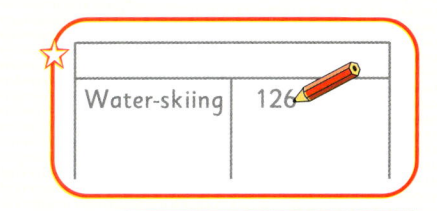

☆ | Water-skiing | 126 |

Breakfast foods	
cereal	27
fruit	19
bacon and egg	26
yoghurt	8
toast	69
kippers	1

2 The hotel manager carried out a survey to find the most popular breakfast foods.

☆ Which was the most popular?

☆ The most popular food was toast.

a Which was more popular, cereal or fruit?

b How many more people chose bacon and egg than yoghurt?

c Which food might the manager take off the menu and why?

Challenge

3 Choose a topic.
Make up a questionnaire with three choices.
Ask eight people in your group or class to give their answers and draw a frequency table to show the results.

Pictograms

Holiday destinations in August

Edinburgh 🧳🧳🧳
London 🧳🧳🧳🧳
Malaga 🧳🧳🧳🧳🧳
Paris 🧳🧳
Orlando 🧳🧳🧳🧳🧳

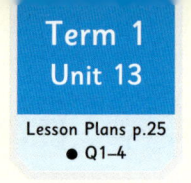

🧳 = 5 people

1 How many people were going to:

 ☆ London? *20 people* ✓

 a Edinburgh?

 b Orlando?

 c Malaga?

2 Which places had the same number of visitors?

3 Which place had most visitors?

Weather for 40 days after St Swithin's day 1924	
rain	30
dry	10

4 Look at the data in the frequency table and use it to make a pictogram where one symbol represents five days.

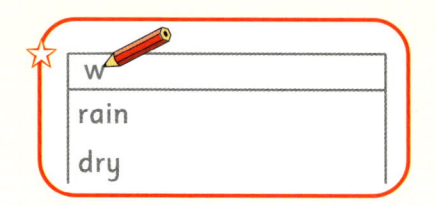

☆
w	
rain	
dry	

Challenge

5 What did you and your friends do last night?

Make a pictogram to show what people did.

Term 1
Unit 13

Lesson Plans p.25
● Q1–4

Interpreting data

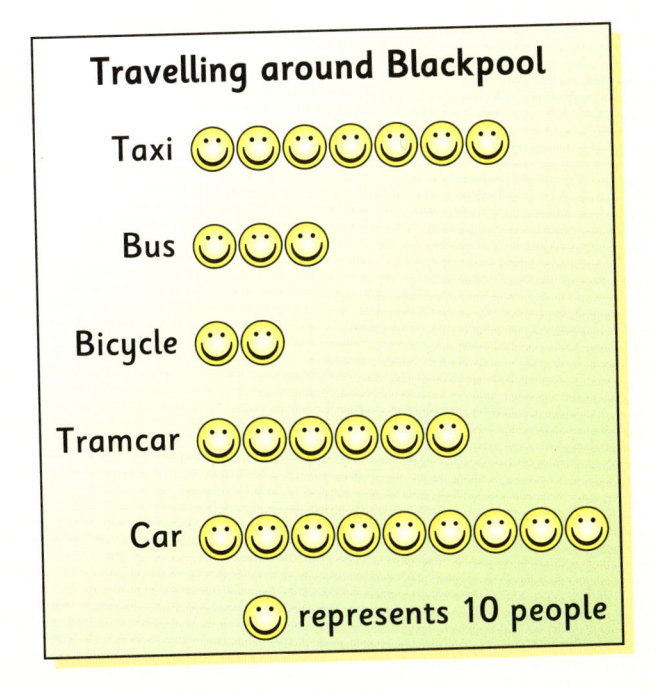

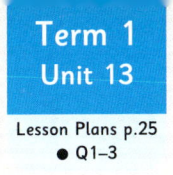

Travelling around Blackpool

Taxi 😊😊😊😊😊😊😊

Bus 😊😊😊

Bicycle 😊😊

Tramcar 😊😊😊😊😊

Car 😊😊😊😊😊😊😊😊😊

😊 represents 10 people

The Blackpool Tourist Board surveyed 270 people to find which type of transport was most popular.

1 How many people travelled by:

☆ taxi?   *(70 people travelled by taxi. ✔)*

a bicycle?   **b** car?

2 How many people, in total, travelled by taxi or tramcar?

3 How many more people travelled by car than by bus?

Challenge

4 Look at your group or class.

Make up a pictogram giving information about either the colour of hair, size of feet or colour of pencil case.

Choose your own symbol and decide whether it should stand for 2, 5, 10 or 20.

Review: addition and subtraction

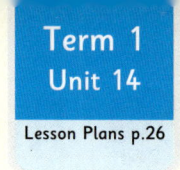

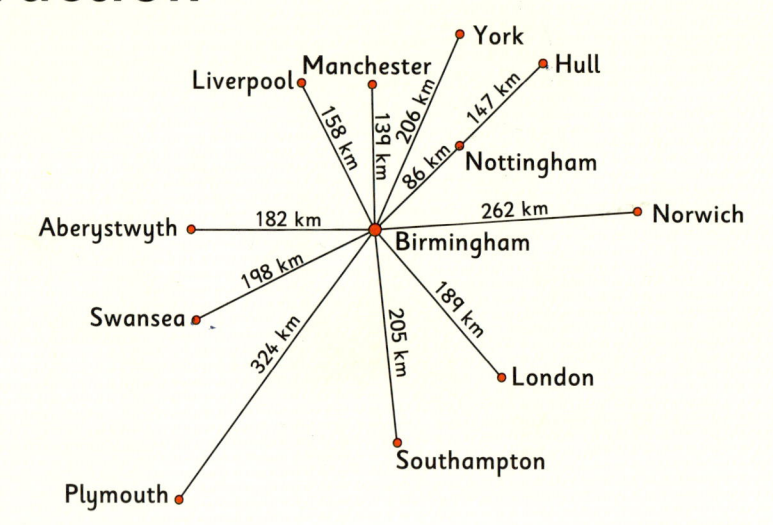

Term 1 Unit 14 — Lesson Plans p.26

Distances (via Birmingham):
- Liverpool 158 km
- Manchester 139 km
- York 206 km
- Hull 147 km
- Nottingham 86 km
- Aberystwyth 182 km
- Norwich 262 km
- Swansea 198 km
- Plymouth 324 km
- London 189 km
- Southampton 205 km

1 Do these mentally. How far is it (via Birmingham) from:

☆ Manchester to Southampton?   205 km + 139 km = 344 km ✓

a Swansea to Norwich?

b York to Southampton?

2 Use a column method. Work out how far it is from:

☆ Nottingham to Plymouth.
```
   86
+ 324
-----
  410
  1 1
``` ✓

a Liverpool to London.   c Swansea to Hull.

b Aberystwyth to Norwich.   d Hull to Southampton.

3 Use a column method. How much further from Birmingham:

a is Norwich than Aberystwyth?   c is Liverpool than Nottingham?

b is Manchester than Nottingham?   d is Plymouth than Norwich?

4 Use a column method. Which is further from Birmingham, and by how much:

☆ Southampton or Liverpool?

Southampton   205
Liverpool   −158
             ―――
              47

Southampton is 47 km further. ✓

a Nottingham or London?   b Plymouth or Hull?

34

Review: choosing the best method

1 Choose whether to work mentally, make jottings or use a written method.

☆ Kites cost £24 each.
What is the cost of 3 kites?

☆ 3 kites at £24
= 3 × £20 + 3 × £4
= £60 + £12
= £72 ✓

a Peter has 63 sweets.
He shares them equally into 4 bags.
How many are left over?

b There are 17 flowers in one bridesmaid's posy.
How many flowers are needed to make 9 posies?

c Lambs are on sale at £4 each.
The farmer spends £72.
How many lambs does he buy?

d 42 paving slabs are needed to make one patio.
How many slabs are needed to make the patios for 6 houses?

e One chair costs £79.
How much will 4 chairs cost?

f There are 6 groups in a class.
The teacher shares 96 crayons equally among the groups.
How many crayons does each group get?

g In the gym store there are 8 boxes.
Each box holds 23 balls.
How many balls altogether?

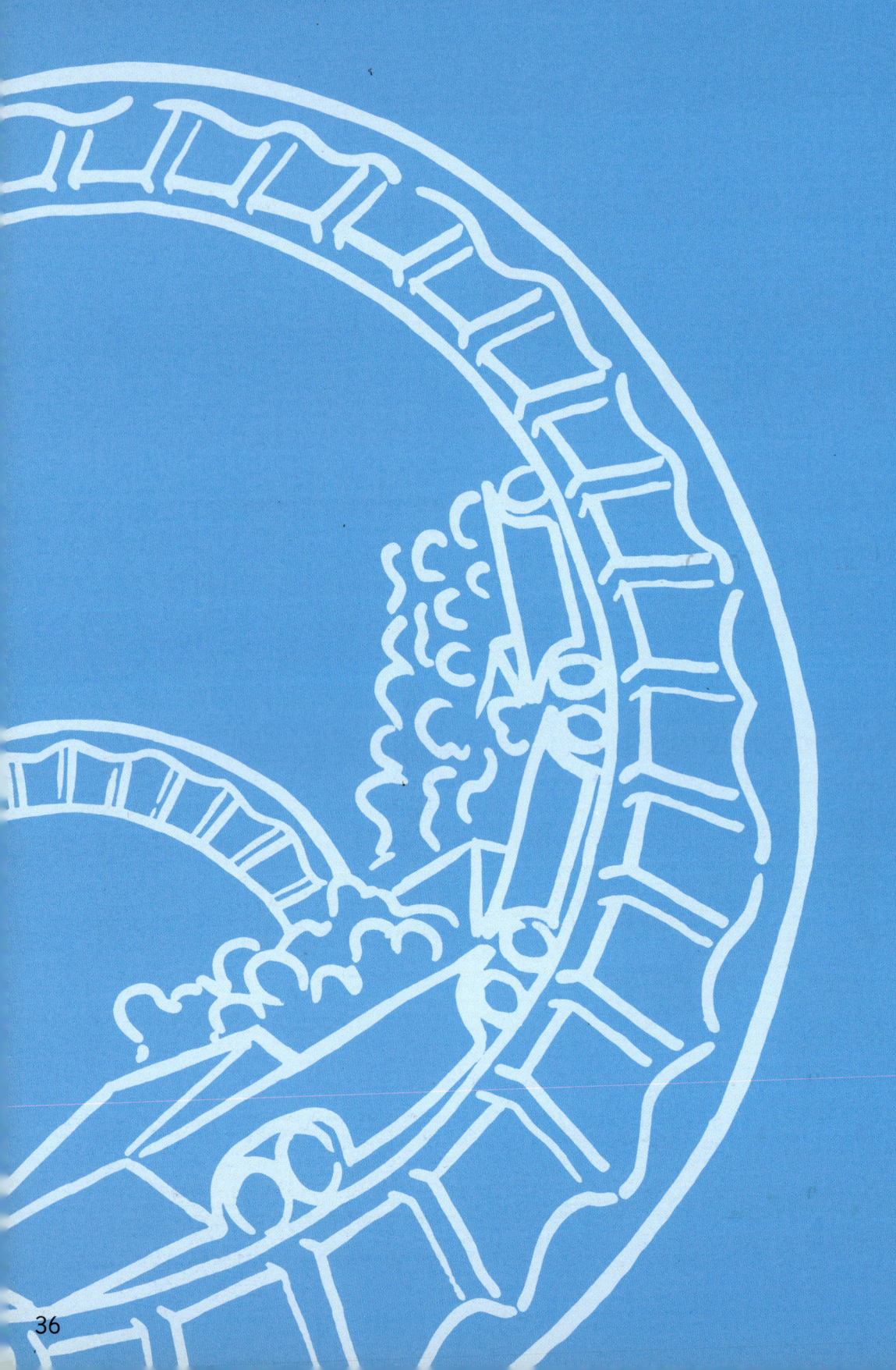

Term 2

Symbols <, >

1 Read the symbols.
Write a number to go in each box.

☆ 42 < ■ < 52   ☆ 42 < 50 < 52   c 872 < ■ < 946

a 78 < ■ < 86   d 938 > ■ > 724   *look carefully*

b 364 < ■ < 521   e 281 > ■ > 218

2 Read the thermometers. Record the temperatures.

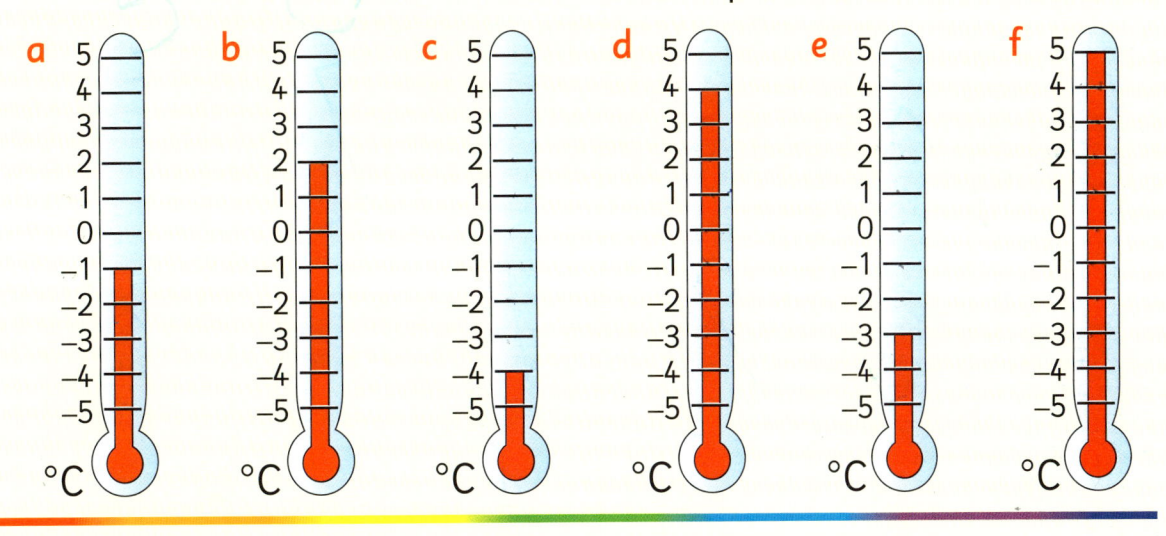

a   b   c   d   e   f
°C °C °C °C °C °C

Challenge

3 What will the new temperatures be if:

thermometer a rises by 2°C ?	thermometer d falls by 7°C ?
thermometer b falls by 4°C ?	thermometer e rises by 5°C ?
thermometer c rises by 7°C ?	thermometer f falls by 8°C ?

Adding multiples of 10

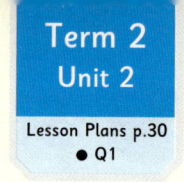

Term 2
Unit 2
Lesson Plans p.30
• Q1

1 **Work out the sums.**
Find pairs that make 100.

> 60 + 20 + 40 =
> 100 + 20 = 120

☆ 60 + 20 + 40 = ☐

a 30 + 80 + 70 = ☐

b 10 + ☐ + 90 = 170

c 20 + 10 + 50 + ☐ = 100

d 40 and double 60 = ☐

e 30 and double 70 = ☐

2 **Look at the dartboards.**
Work out the totals.
Show your workings.

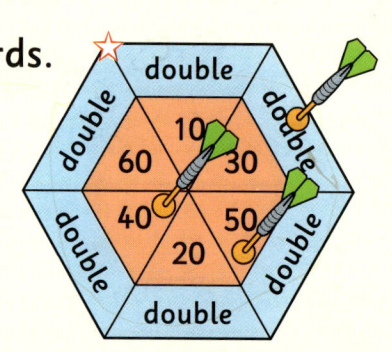

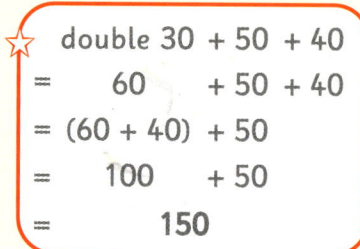

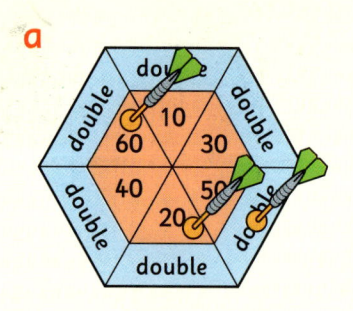

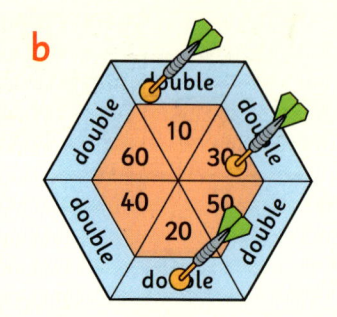

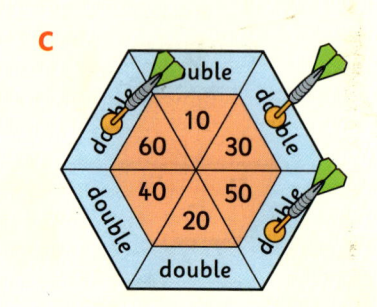

> ☆ double 30 + 50 + 40
> =   60   + 50 + 40
> = (60 + 40) + 50
> =   100   + 50
> =   150

a

b

c

Challenge

3 Find different ways of scoring a total of 120 with three darts.

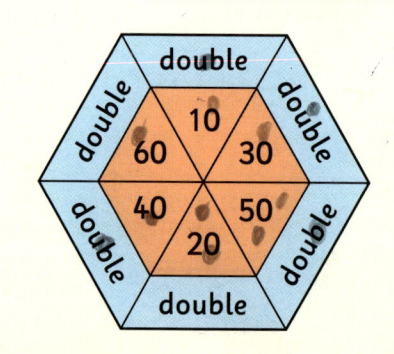

38

Partitioning

Term 2 Unit 2
Lesson Plans p.31
● Q1

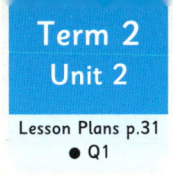

1 Add or subtract using partitioning.

   a 65 + 34 =   **b** 33 + 58 =   **c** 56 − 39 =

---

2 Which two board numbers add to make each score?
Show your workings.

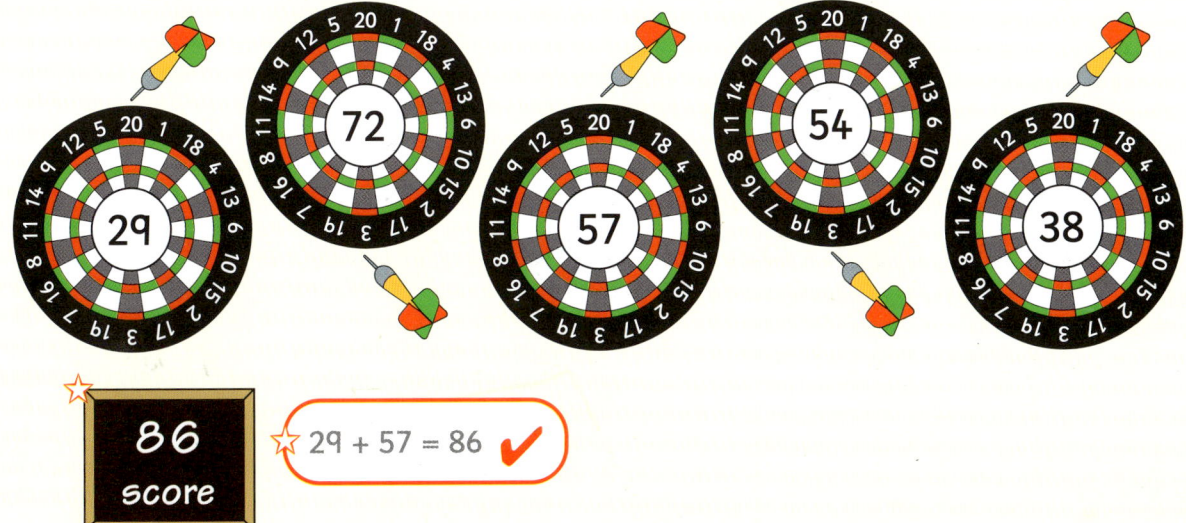

Dartboards: 29, 72, 57, 54, 38

★ 86 score   ★ 29 + 57 = 86 ✓

a 95 score   **b** 83 score   **c** 92 score   **d** 111 score   **e** 126 score

---

Challenge

3 Add the scores on the dartboards.
Subtract each from 101.

a   **b**   **c**

39

Word problems

Fact: Six children from a junior school in the Midlands created a World record for throwing pennies into a plastic bucket from a distance of three metres. They collected £10.00 in pennies in exactly 11 minutes.

Two teams from another school had their own competition. After 5 minutes these were the results.

Team A	
Zoe	53p
Salma	24p
Max	30p

Team B	
Rob	39p
Eva	22p
Peter	80p

1 Work out the problems.

☆ How much did Zoe and Salma get into the bucket altogether?

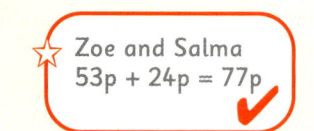

> Zoe and Salma
> 53p + 24p = 77p ✓

a How much did Team A get into their bucket?

b How much did Zoe, Rob and Eva get altogether?

c How much more would Eva need to have the same as Salma?

d How many pennies do you think Salma might throw in 10 minutes?

e What is the difference between Team A's total and Team B's?

Challenge

2 Both teams carry on for another 5 minutes. How far short of £10.00 do you think they will be then?

Solving problems

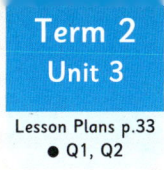

Term 2 Unit 3
Lesson Plans p.33
• Q1, Q2

Games and prices: draughts 65p, chess £1.20, dartboard £2.00, dominoes £1.15, cards 99p

1 Addition problems

☆ Which two games cost £2.35 altogether?

> chess   dominoes
> £1.20 + £1.15 = £2.35 ✓

a Eva bought three games, the total was £3.00. Which games did she buy?

b I want to buy three games. What is the most I could spend? What is the least I could spend?

2 Subtraction problems

☆ How much more than the cards are the dominoes?

> £1.15 – 99p = 16p ✓

a What is the difference in price between the most expensive and the least expensive game?

b How much change will I get from £2.00 if I buy dominoes?

3 Two-step problems

☆ I bought a chess set and a pack of cards. How much change did I get from £5.00?

> £1.20 + 99p = £2.19
> £5.00 – £2.19 = £2.81 ✓

a I bought three games. My change from £5.00 was £1.15, which games did I buy?

b I want to buy three games. What is the most change I can get from £5.00? What is the least?

Challenge

4 Eva had £2.00 more than Max, who had £3.00 less than Jim. How much did Jim have if Eva had £10.00?

Measuring angles

1 Which is the larger angle? ☆ P ✓

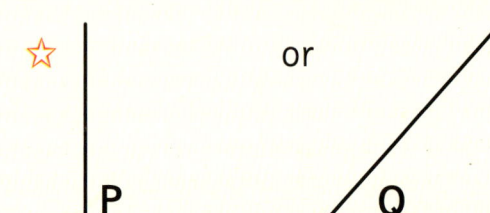

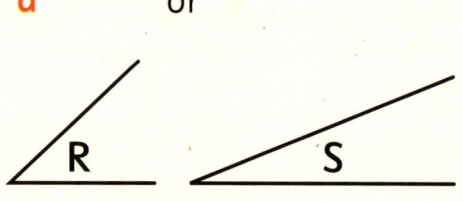

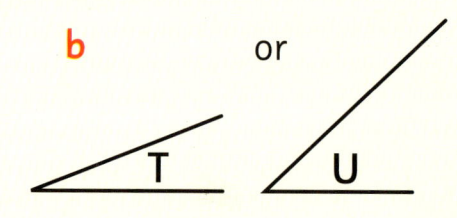

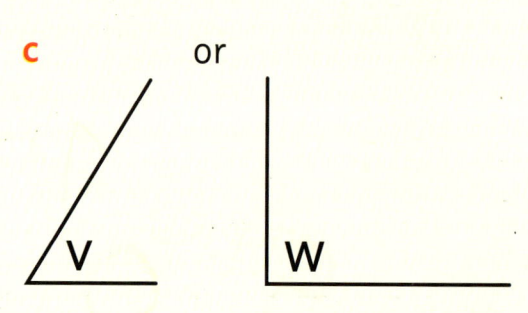

☆ P or Q

a R or S

b T or U

c V or W

2 Using a set square, draw and label these angles.

☆ 90°

a 60°
b 45°
c 30°

☆ 90° ✓

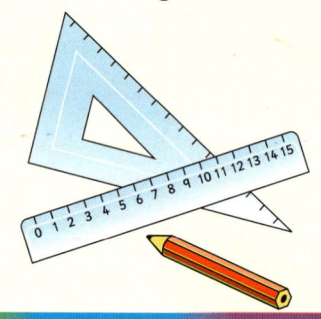

Challenge

3 Identify the angles marked **a**, **b** and **c**. Draw these shapes making sure the angles are the correct size.

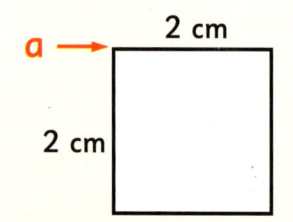

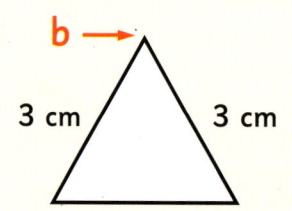

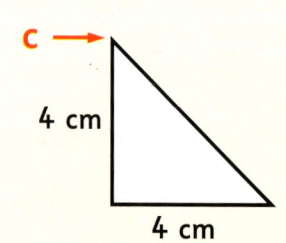

a → 2 cm, 2 cm (square)

b → 3 cm, 3 cm (triangle)

c → 4 cm, 4 cm (triangle)

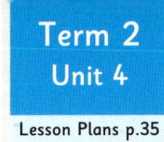

Compass directions

Term 2 Unit 4
Lesson Plans p.35
• Q1

1 Write the directions to help Rob to find his way around the supermarket and fill his trolley.

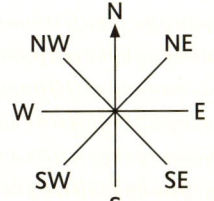

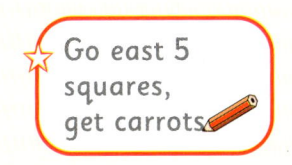

☆ Go east 5 squares, get carrots

Challenge

2 **Rob has left his wallet behind.** Write directions for Rob's journey back through the supermarket.

Shapes and nets

Term 2 Unit 5
Lesson Plans p.36
● Q1, 2

1 Match the net to the 3D shape.

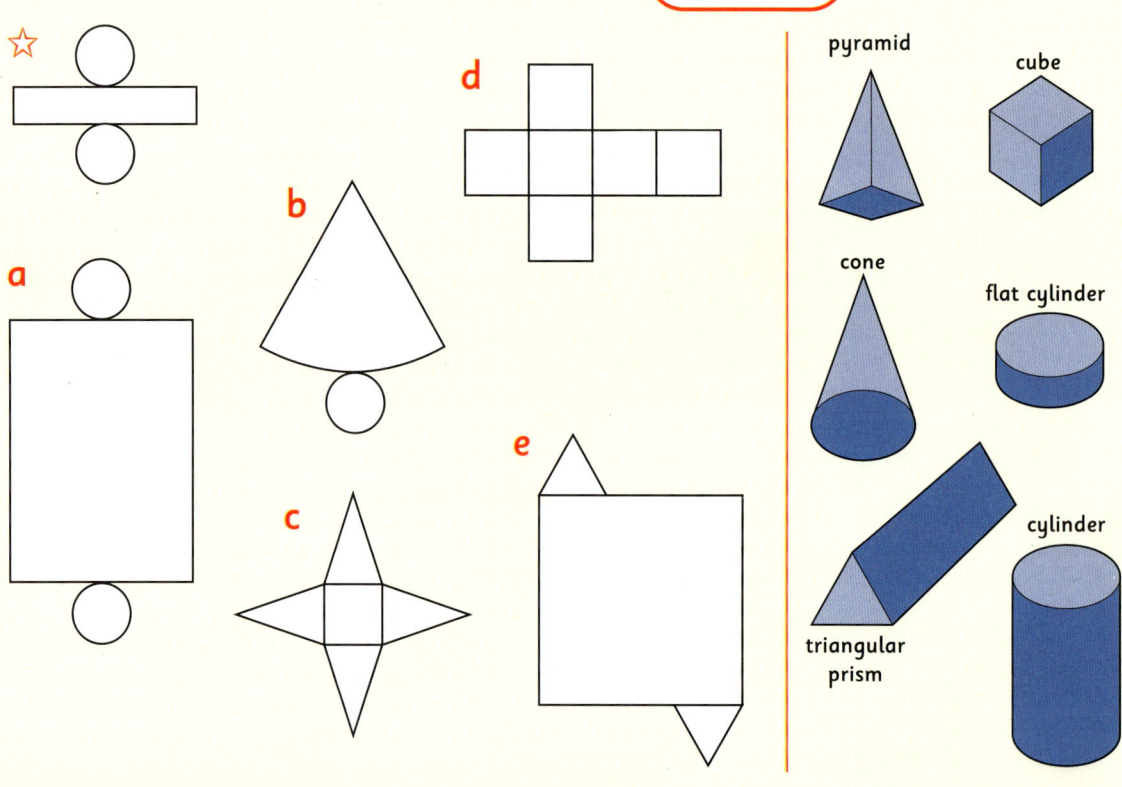

flat cylinder ✓

pyramid
cube
cone
flat cylinder
triangular prism
cylinder

2 How many cubes in each shape?

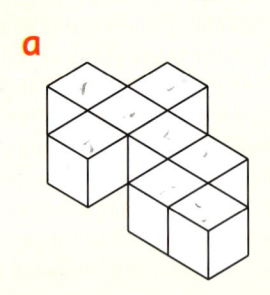

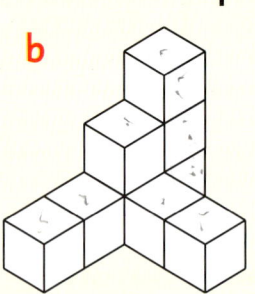

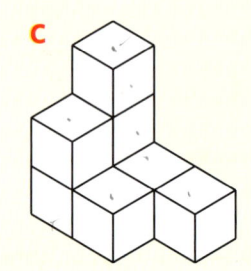

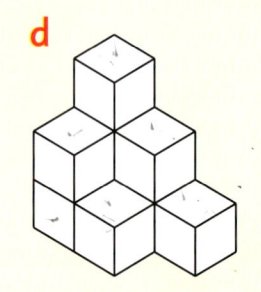

a   b   c   d

Challenge

3 Make a shape using Multilink cubes then draw it.

44

Area

1 What is the area of each shape?

Each side of each square is one centimetre.

☆ 12 cm² ✓

2 Each square is 1 cm². What area is shaded in each picture?

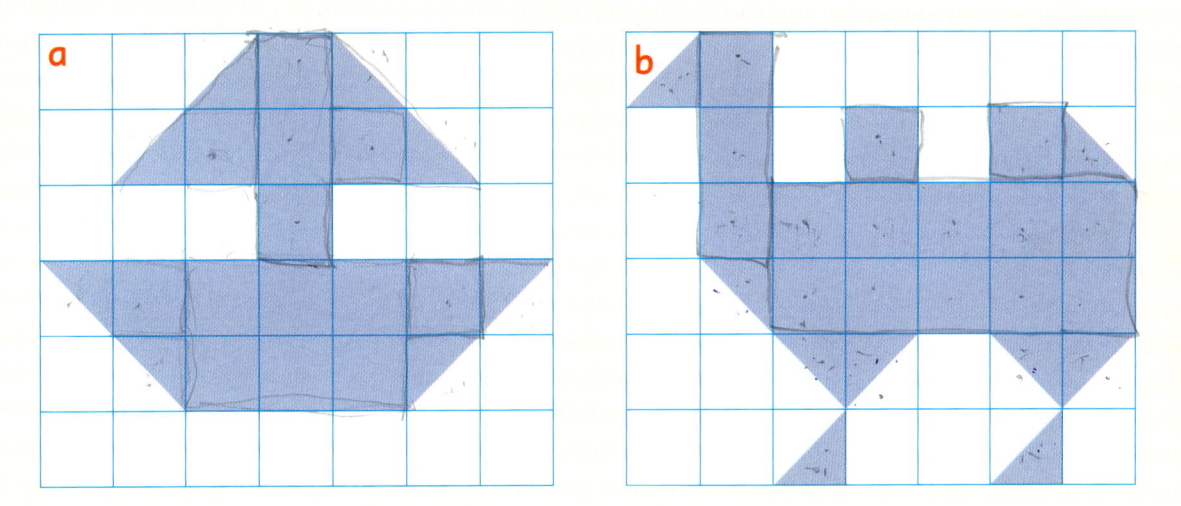

Challenge

3 Draw a picture on squared paper with an area of between 20 cm² and 30 cm².

What is your estimate of its actual area?

Estimating mass

1 Choose the best estimate for each object.

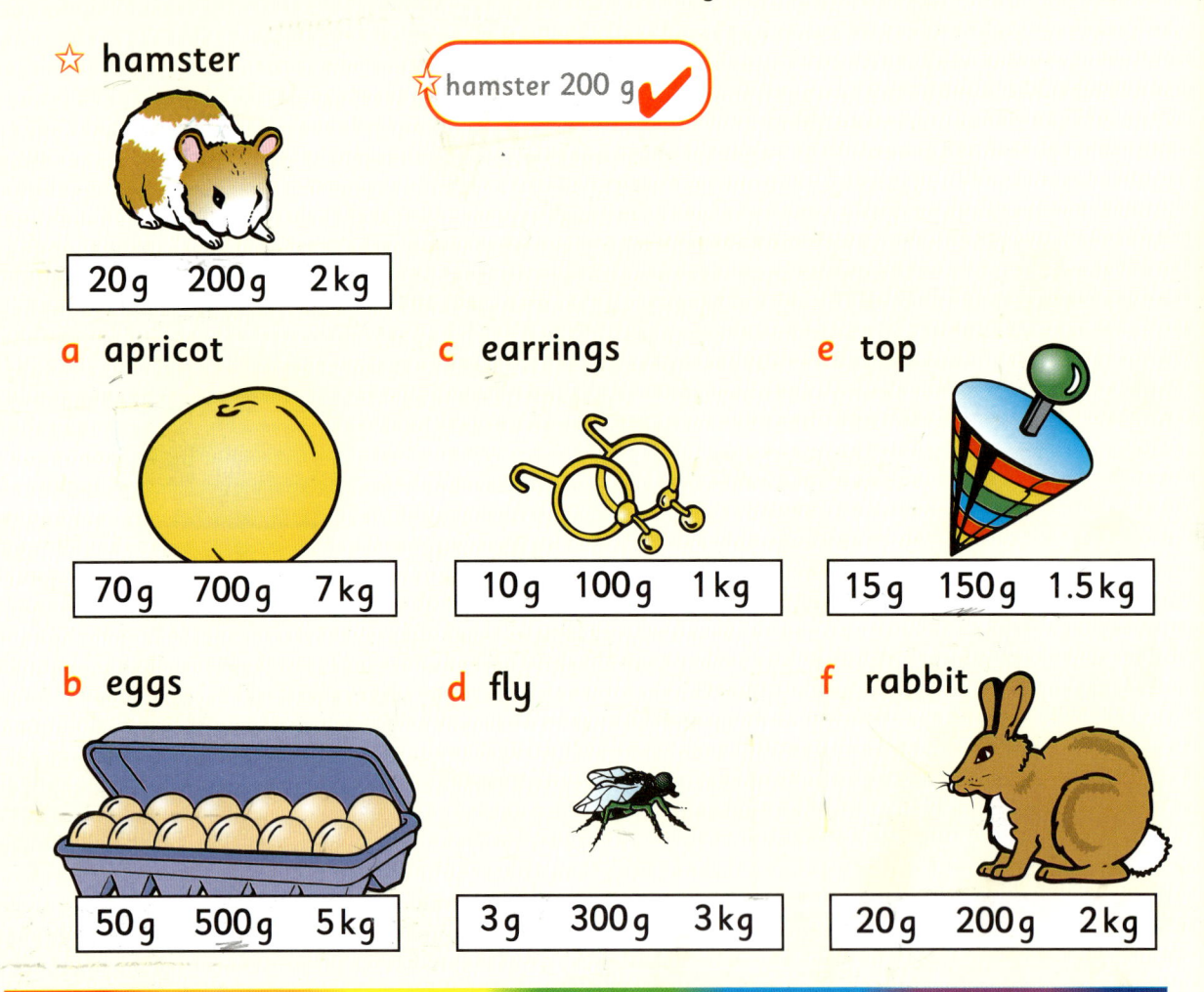

☆ hamster

20 g   200 g   2 kg

☆ hamster 200 g ✓

a apricot

70 g   700 g   7 kg

c earrings

10 g   100 g   1 kg

e top

15 g   150 g   1.5 kg

b eggs

50 g   500 g   5 kg

d fly

3 g   300 g   3 kg

f rabbit

20 g   200 g   2 kg

2 Order the objects from lightest to heaviest.

☆ 3 g f

Use the first letter from the name of each object, including the hamster, to spell the name of a very light object.

Challenge

3 Find some objects in the classroom that weigh as close as possible to: 500 g
50 g

Kilograms

Term 2 Unit 6
Lesson Plans p.38
● Q1

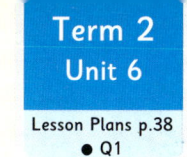

1 a Follow the path with your finger. Choose one weight in each circle to give you the lightest shopping.

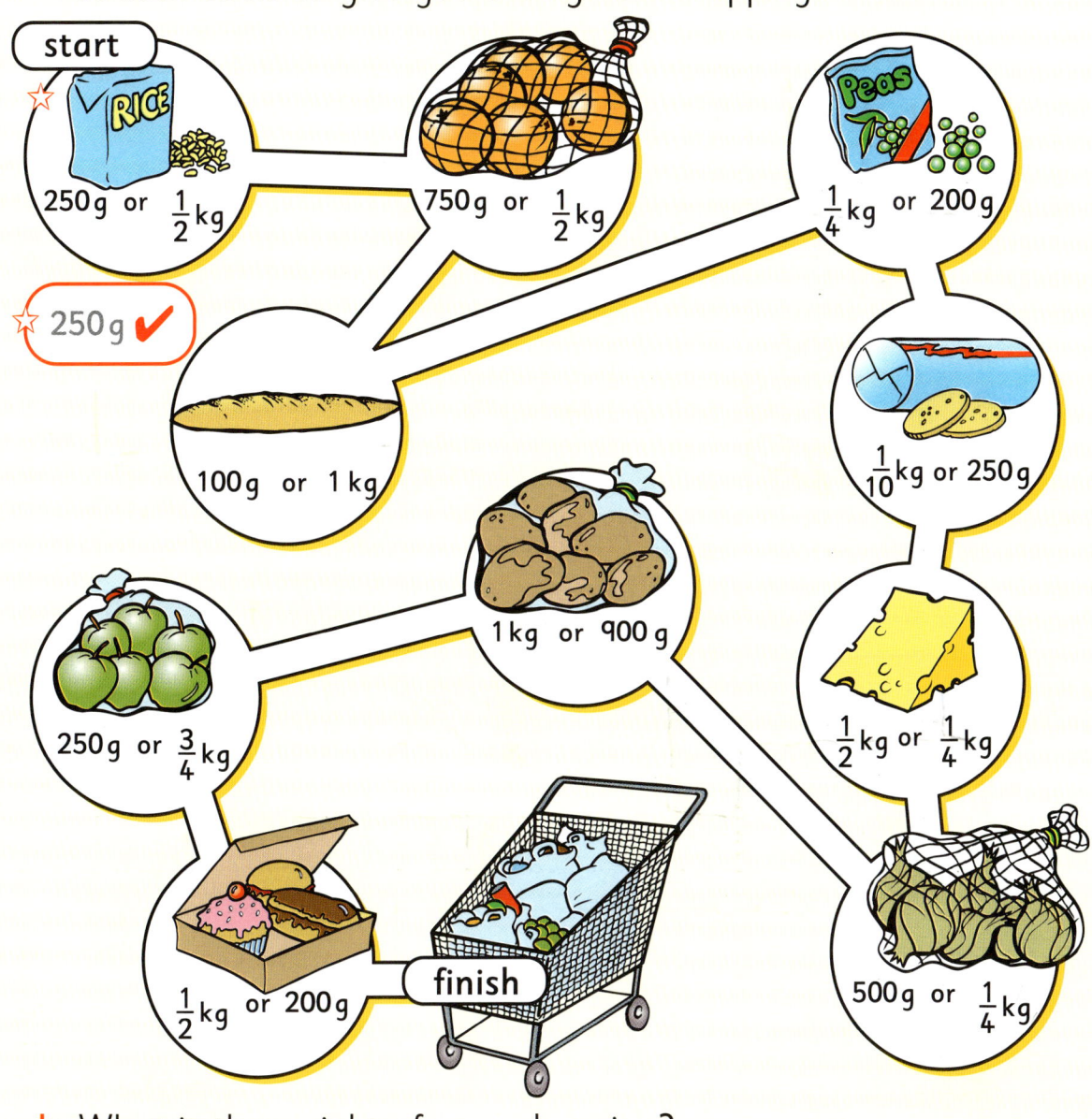

start

250 g or ½ kg

750 g or ½ kg

¼ kg or 200 g

250 g ✓

100 g or 1 kg

⅒ kg or 250 g

250 g or ¾ kg

1 kg or 900 g

½ kg or ¼ kg

½ kg or 200 g

finish

500 g or ¼ kg

b What is the weight of your shopping?

Challenge

2 Add up the heaviest weights in each circle to find the total weight of the heaviest shopping.

47

Review: ordering and rounding

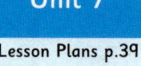

Term 2 Unit 7
Lesson Plans p.39

1 Put these numbers in order, smallest first.

a 8437   ☆ 3487   4738   8374   3784

☆ 3487, ✏️

b 2061   2106   1260   1026   1620

c 5447   4574   4475   7454   4457

2 Use the same digits. Write a number that works for these:

☆ 3748 < ■■■■ < 4783   b 5910 < ■■■■ < 9510

☆ 3784 ✔

a 6254 > ■■■■ > 2645   c 5412 > ■■■■ > 4251

3 Round each number to the nearest 10 and 100.

☆ 738   b 633   d 265

☆ 740, 700 ✔

a 459   c 512   e 972

48

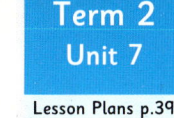

Review: word problems

1 **Read the problems.** Show your working. Write the answers.

☆ A spider has 8 legs.
How many legs on 3 spiders?
How many on 10 spiders?

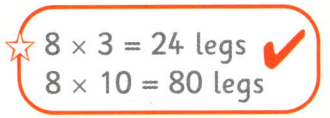

☆ 8 × 3 = 24 legs ✓
8 × 10 = 80 legs

a There are 24 cakes on a tray.
Half of the cakes are chocolate.
A third of the chocolate cakes have Smarties on them.
How many have Smarties?

b There are five shelves of books.
Three shelves have 15 books.
One shelf has 10 books and one shelf has five.
How many books altogether?

c Salma weighs 750 g more than Zoe. Zoe weighs 32.5 kg.
How much does Salma weigh?

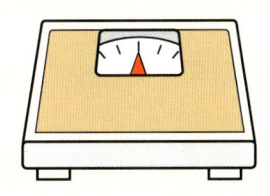

d An apple has a mass of about 150 g. Roughly how many apples in a 1 kg bag? What is the mass of 20 apples?

e Steve has a bag of twelve 20p coins. He shares them equally between four people. How much money does each person have? How much altogether?

f Eva is having a party. Change this pizza recipe for 4 people to a recipe for 8 people.

250 g flour
50 g fat
125 g cheese
2 tomatoes
200 g pineapple chunks

Term 2 Unit 7
Lesson Plans p.39

Number steps

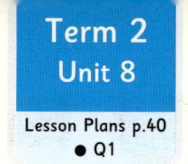

Term 2 Unit 8
Lesson Plans p.40
● Q1

1 Write out the number sequence.

36   41   46   ▪   56   ▪

☆ 36, 41, 46, 51, 56, 61 ✓

a 7, 10, ▪, 16, 19, ▪, ▪, 28

b 37, 33, 29, ▪, ▪, 17, ▪, 9

c 35, 45, ▪, 65, 75, ▪, ▪, 105

2 Spot the steps!

☆ 2, 5, 8, 11, 14, 17   Steps of 3. ✓

a 6, 11, 16, 21, 26, 31

b 60, 48, 36, 24, 12, 0

3 Carry on…!

☆ 7, 11, 15, 19, ▪, ▪, ▪, ▪   ☆ 7, 11, 15, 19, 23, 27, 31, 35 ✓

a 8, 14, 20, 26, ▪, ▪, ▪, ▪

b 40, 38, 36, 34, ▪, ▪, ▪, ▪

Challenge

4 Write a number sequence with six numbers.
The last number must be 48.
How many different sequences can you make?

50

Number sequences

Term 2 Unit 8
Lesson Plans p.41
● Q1, 2

1 Find the rule and carry on.

☆ −2, −4, −6, −8, ■, ■, ■   ☆ −2, −4, −6, −8, −10, −12, −14 ✓

a 15, 10, 5, 0, ■, ■, ■

b −10, −8, −6, −4, ■, ■, ■

c 11, 9, 7, 5, ■, ■, ■

d 0, −3, −6, −9, ■, ■, ■

2 Complete the number sequence.

☆ 4, 2, ■, ■, −4, ■   ☆ 4, 2, 0, −2, −4, −6 ✓

a ■, ■, 10, 5, ■, ■, −10

b ■, 16, 8, ■, ■, −16

c −18, −12, ■, 0, ■, ■

3 Explain the rule.

☆ −10, −5, 0, 5, 10, 15, 20   ☆ Count on in 5s. ✓

a 36, 25, 14, 3, −8, −19, −30

b −24, −16, −8, 0, 8, 16, 24

c 39, 30, 21, 12, 3, −6, −15

Challenge

4 How many different number sequences can you make which start with −16 and end in 16?

51

Multiplying by 9 and 11

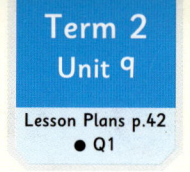

Term 2 Unit 9
Lesson Plans p.42
• Q1

1 Multiply by 11. Choose the correct answer from the boxes.

☆ 12 × 11 = | 352 |

a 41 × 11 = | 297 |

b 32 × 11 = | 451 |

c 27 × 11 = ☆| 132 |

☆ 12 × 11
12 × 10 → 120
     +   12
        ———
        132
12 × 11 = 132 ✔

---

2 Write the sum and its answer.

a 18 × 11 = ■   c 14 × 11 = ■   e 16 × 11 = ■

b 30 × 11 = ■   d 20 × 11 = ■   f 19 × 11 = ■

---

3 Multiply by 9, using ×10 to help you.

☆ 6 × 9 = ■   c 3 × 9 = ■

a 14 × 9 = ■   d 13 × 9 = ■

b 8 × 9 = ■   e 18 × 9 = ■

☆ 6 × 9
6 × 10 → 60
     −   6
        ——
        54
6 × 9 = 54 ✔

Challenge

4 Write a sum with an answer of 9.

[   ] ÷ [   ] = 9

What are the smallest numbers you can think of to go in the boxes? What are the largest?

52

Theme Park food problems

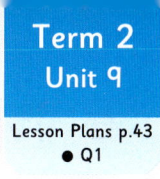

Term 2 Unit 9
Lesson Plans p.43
• Q1

- Sandwich (cheese): £1.05
- Crisps: 30p
- Chips: 70p
- Cola: 50p
- Burger: £1.20
- Doughnuts: 40p
- Ice cream: £1.20

Solve these problems. Show your working.

1 ☆ How much do burger and chips cost?

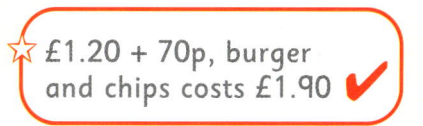

> ☆ £1.20 + 70p, burger and chips costs £1.90 ✓

   a Anna and Rob have burger and chips, Mum and Dad have a burger. Everyone has a cola. How much is the bill?

   b Dad pays with a £20 note. How much change should he get?

2 a A family of five order colas and ice creams for everyone. What is the cost?

   b How much change will there be from £10?

3 Two adults and two children go to the Theme Park. The total cost is £70. Children's tickets cost £15 each. How much do adults pay?

Challenge

4 You have £5 to spend on lunch for two people. What different combinations can you make spending £5 or less each time?

53

Term 2 Unit 10
Lesson Plans p.45
● Q1

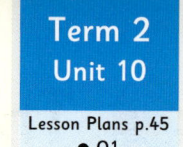

Dividing pounds

1 **How much each?** Share each amount between:
   2 children
   4 children
   5 children
   10 children

   ☆ 2 children have £7.50
   4 children have £3.75
   5 children have £3.00
   10 children have £1.50 ✔

☆   a   b   c

---

2 ☆ Four children have £5 to share. How much will each child have?

   ☆ £5 ÷ 4 = £1.25
   Each child has £1.25 ✔

   a Anna and Steve have exactly the same pocket money each week. Altogether it costs their parents £6.50. How much does each child have?

   b Peter is saving for a CD which costs £13.50. He saves £2.25 pocket money each week. How many weeks will he have to save?

Challenge

3 **a** The money in my money box could be divided equally between 2, 4, 5 or 10 people giving each one a whole number of pounds. What is the least I could have in my money box?

   b Find three more amounts that could be in my money box.

Theme Park ride problems

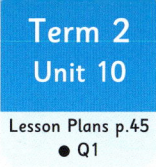

Term 2
Unit 10

Lesson Plans p.45
• Q1

Solve these problems.
Show your working.

☆ **Forty-two people are queuing for the Corkscrew ride.** Thirty-seven more join the queue and sixteen get on the ride. How many in the queue?

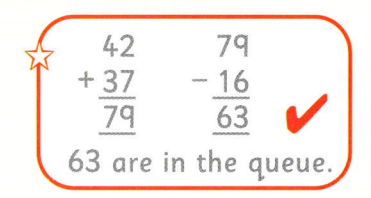

```
   42        79
 + 37      - 16
   ——        ——
   79        63   ✓
```
63 are in the queue.

1 **The Oblivion ride has seven cars.** Each car carries sixteen people. Five cars are full but two cars have only fourteen people in them. How many people will ride?

2 **The Corkscrew has a quarter of the number queuing for the Oblivion ride.** The Oblivion ride has 56 people in its queue. How many are queuing for the Corkscrew?

3 **The Tea Cups ride has twelve gondolas and each one seats five people.** If the ride operates twenty times an hour, how many people can ride each hour?

Challenge

4 Make up a word problem that uses more than one number operation.

Matching fractions

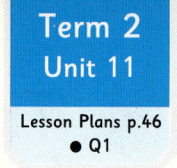

Term 2 Unit 11
Lesson Plans p.46
• Q1

1. Write two fractions to match each picture.

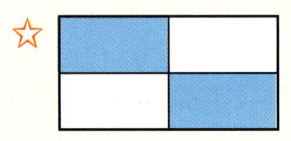

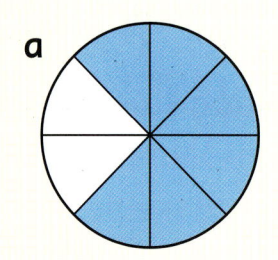

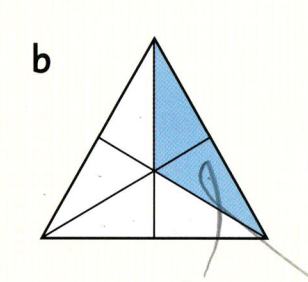

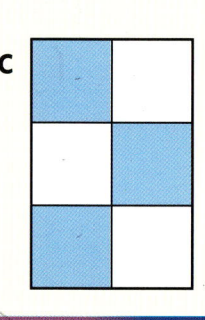

☆ $\frac{2}{4}, \frac{1}{2}$ ✓

a   b   c

2. Greater or less than $\frac{1}{2}$?

☆ $\frac{6}{10}$ a $\frac{4}{6}$ b $\frac{1}{8}$ c $\frac{7}{8}$ d $\frac{2}{3}$ e $\frac{2}{6}$

☆ $\frac{6}{10}$ is greater than $\frac{1}{2}$ ✓

3. Match the pairs that make 1.

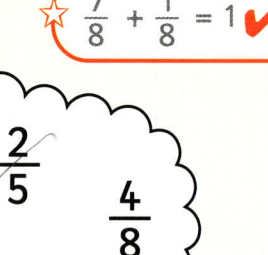

☆ $\frac{7}{8} + \frac{1}{8} = 1$ ✓

$\frac{7}{10}$, $\frac{1}{4}$, $\frac{1}{2}$, $\frac{3}{6}$, ☆$\frac{1}{8}$, $\frac{2}{3}$, $\frac{2}{5}$, ☆$\frac{7}{8}$, $\frac{5}{10}$, $\frac{1}{3}$, $\frac{3}{4}$, $\frac{3}{10}$, $\frac{3}{5}$, $\frac{4}{8}$

Challenge

4. Can you find six different ways to make 1, using three fractions each time?

$\frac{\blacksquare}{\blacksquare} + \frac{\blacksquare}{\blacksquare} + \frac{\blacksquare}{\blacksquare} = 1$

Paying for pizza

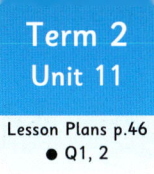

Mamma Mia Pizza Parlour

		Extra Toppings			
small	£3.50	cheese	40p	mushrooms	35p
medium	£3.75	tomatoes	30p	salami	55p
large	£4.00	peppers	50p	prawns	70p
				tuna	65p
		peppers	50p		

☆ Dad orders a large pizza with extra cheese. How much does he pay?

> pizza £4.00
> cheese 0.40
> _____
> £4.40
> He pays £4.40. ✓

1 Zoe's family order one of each size pizza and each pizza has extra cheese. How much is the bill?

2 How much would you pay for a medium pizza with extra peppers and mushrooms?

3 Zoe orders a small pizza with extra peppers and cheese. How much does she pay?

4 How much would you pay for the cheapest pizza with the most expensive extra topping?

Challenge

5 My pizza bill is more than £4 but less than £4.50.
I chose two extra toppings.
Find three combinations I might have ordered!

Using decimals

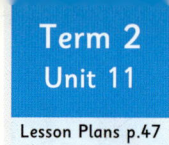

☆ The bill is £17.20.
Mum pays with a £20 note.
How much change?

☆ £20 – £17.20 = £2.80
He has £2.80 change. ✓

1 Zoe's family eat four pizzas at £3.50 each and their extra toppings cost £1.40.
How much is their bill?

2 The tables at Mamma Mia's are 90 cm long and 90 cm wide.
The tablecloths overhang by 20 cm at each side.
How wide are the tablecloths?
Write your answer in centimetres and metres.

3 For Zoe's birthday treat, they put three tables together in a line.
How many metres long is the birthday table?

4 Zoe's birthday treat at Mamma Mia's costs £42.30 plus £15 for a special cake.
How much change from £60?

Challenge

5 I pay my bill with two £10 notes and two £2 coins.
I get £1.93 change. How much was my bill?

Term 2 Unit 11
Lesson Plans p.47
● Q1, 2

Using bar charts (1)

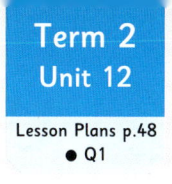

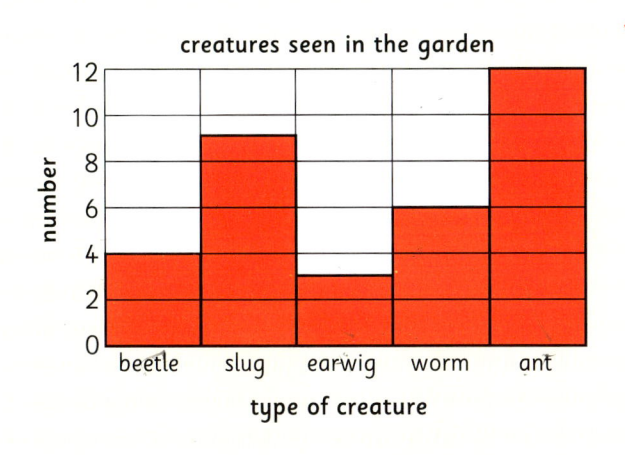

1 In the garden: ⭐ 4 ✓

creatures seen in the garden

☆ how many beetles were seen?

a how many slugs were seen?

b how many more ants than worms were found?

c altogether how many creepy creatures were seen?

2 In the garden: ⭐ 15 ✓

☆ how many more finches than jays were seen?

a how many finches and bluetits were seen altogether?

b how many thrushes were seen?

c how many birds were seen altogether?

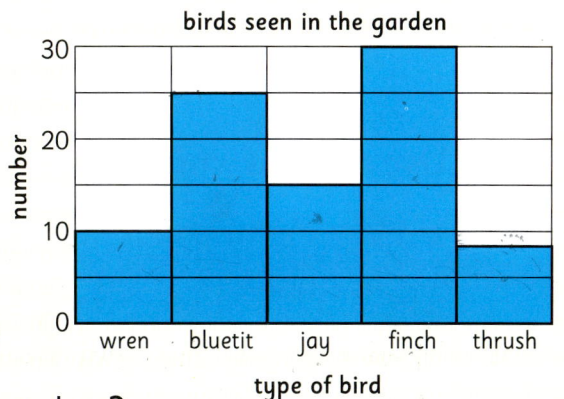

3 Show the information in this frequency table on a bar chart.

flower	rose	crocus	daisy	tulip	lupin
number found in the garden	10	12	8	7	15

Challenge

4 a Look at a newspaper or look on the Internet to find the temperatures of some foreign cities.

b Construct a bar chart to show what you have found.

Using bar charts (2)

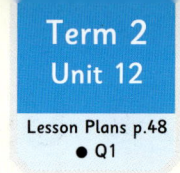

Here is some information about the children in Class 4B at Wurcard Primary School.

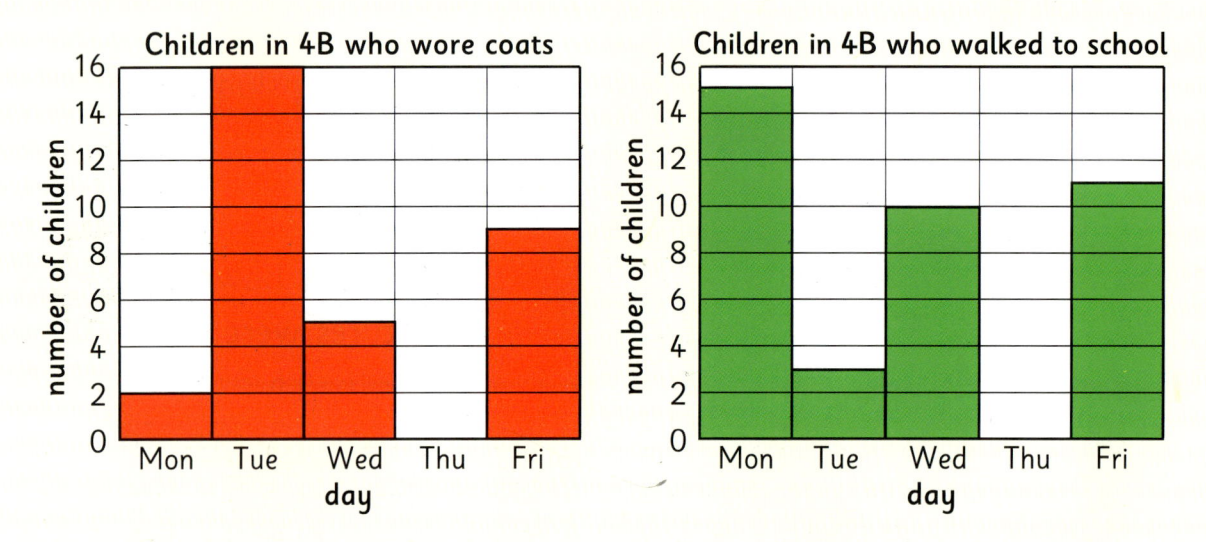

Children in 4B who wore coats

Children in 4B who walked to school

1 Use the bar charts to answer the questions.

☆ How many children in Class 4B walked to school on Tuesday?   ☆ 3 ✓

a How many children walked to school on Thursday?

b How many more children wore coats on Tuesday than on Monday?

c Which day do you think was the coldest day of the week? Explain your answer.

d Which day do you think was the warmest day of the week? Explain your answer.

e Why do you think happened on Thursday?

60

Using bar charts (3)

Here is some information about how the children travel to school on dry days and on wet days.

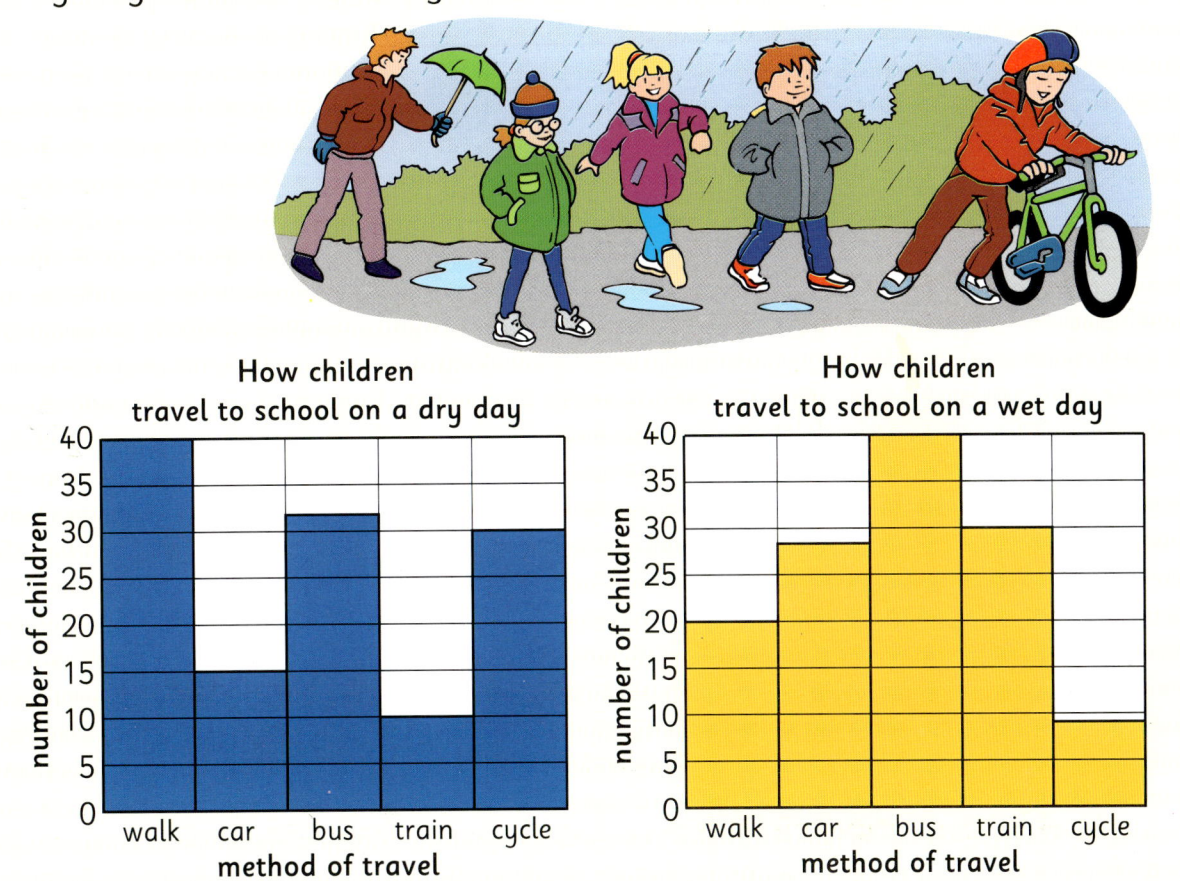

1 Look at the bar charts to answer these questions.

☆ How many more children walk on a dry day than on a wet day?

☆ 20 ✓

a How many children travel by car on a wet day?

b How many children catch the bus on a dry day?

c How many fewer children cycle on a wet day than on a dry day?

Challenge

2 Make up some questions of your own to ask your partner.

Review: multiplication and division facts

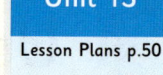

Term 2 Unit 13
Lesson Plans p.50

1 Use three of these numbers each time.
Multiply them together.
Can you find nine different products?

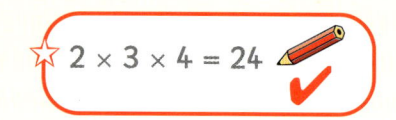

☆ 2 × 3 × 4 = 24 ✓

3   5
2   4   10

2 Write the answers.

☆ How many fours in 44?

☆ 11 ✓

a Share 27 between 9.
b Divide 36 by 4.
c Half of 15.
d One third of 12.
e 32 ÷ 4 = ■
f Half of 38.
g 160 divided by 80.

3 Number cruncher

Work along the row multiplying and dividing.
What is the final answer?

a ☆ 10 × 6 ÷ 5 × 2 ÷ 3 × 10 ÷ 2 × 0 =   ☆ 60, 12
b 5 × 6 ÷ 3 × 2 ÷ 5 × 4 ÷ 8 × 1 =

Review: equivalent fractions

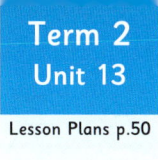

1 Write two fractions for each ringed set. $\frac{2}{8}, \frac{1}{4}$ ✓

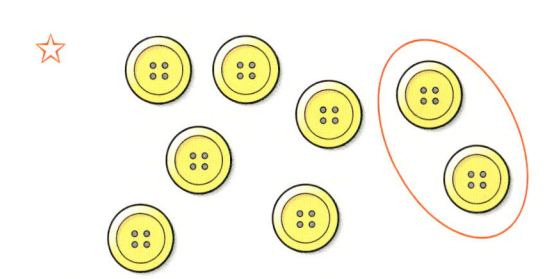

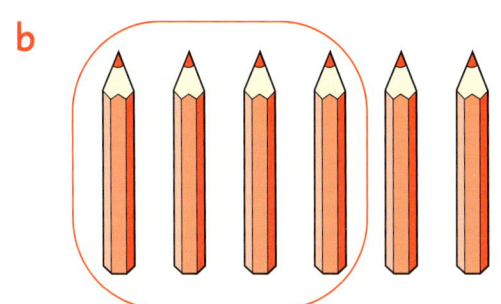

a

b

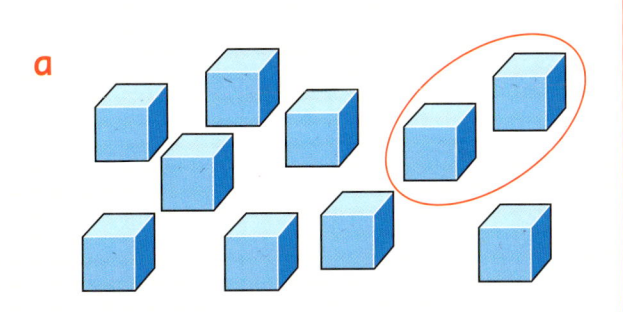

c

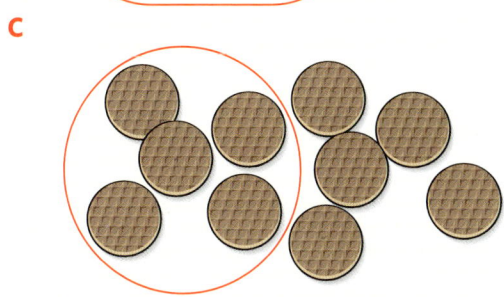

2 Write two fractions for each shaded area. $\frac{5}{10}, \frac{1}{2}$ ✓

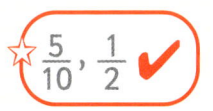

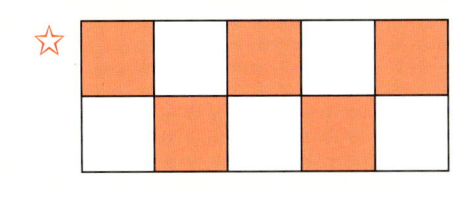

a

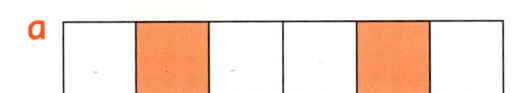

b

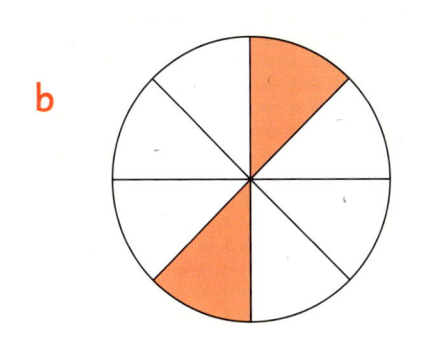

c

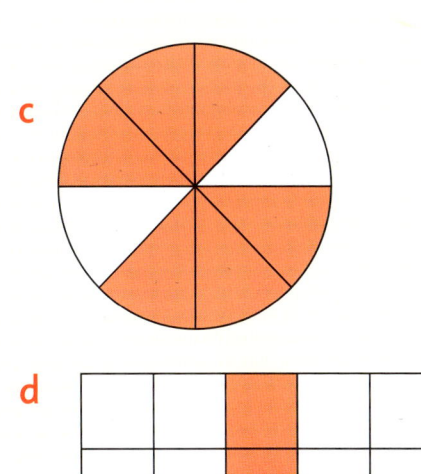

d

Term 3

Multiplying by 10 and 100

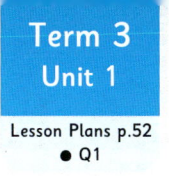

Term 3 Unit 1
Lesson Plans p.52
• Q1

1 Multiply each number by 1, 10 and 100.

Look at the pattern in each set.

☆ 7

```
7 ×   1 =   7
7 ×  10 =  70
7 × 100 = 700
```

a 12
b 15
c 24

d 35
e 47
f 49

---

2 Copy the tables. Write the numbers that come out of the machine.

a ×10 machine

in	16	34	29	56	41	70
out	160					

b ×100 machine

in	13	28	22	40	53	39
out						

Challenge

3 Press these keys on a calculator.

`1` `0` `×` `2` `=` `=` `=`

What is happening to the answer each time?

Change the 2 for a different number.

Try making a ×100 machine.

Mental addition

Term 3 Unit 2
Lesson Plans p.54
● Q1

Pop ice 40p
Cone 80p
Flake 25p
Chipchoc 92p
Minicool 34p

1 How much altogether?

Work out the cost in your head and write down each total.

☆ Cone and Minicool — 114p or £1.14 ✓ **b** Cone and flake

a Pop ice and Minicool **c** Chipchoc and Pop ice

2 Copy and answer each of these using a mental method.

a 46 + 29 **d** 61 + 34 **g** 62 + 38

b 39 + 54 **e** 28 + 57 **h** 47 + 74

c 58 + 45 **f** 79 + 43 **i** 59 + 62

Challenge

3 Copy and complete the pyramid sums like this.

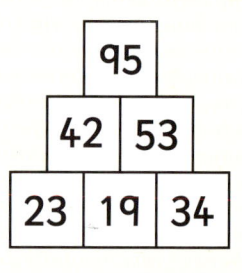

Make **b** and **c** different.

	95	
42		53
23	19	34

a 26 18 37

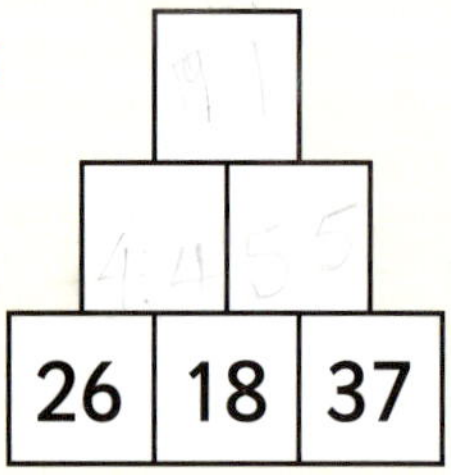

b 100

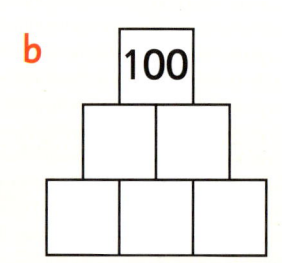

c 100

66

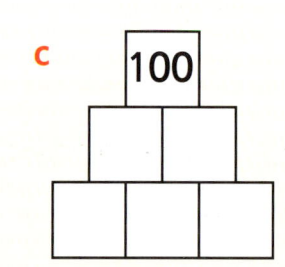

Mental subtraction

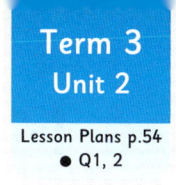

Term 3 Unit 2
Lesson Plans p.54
• Q1, 2

1 How much has Dad got left?

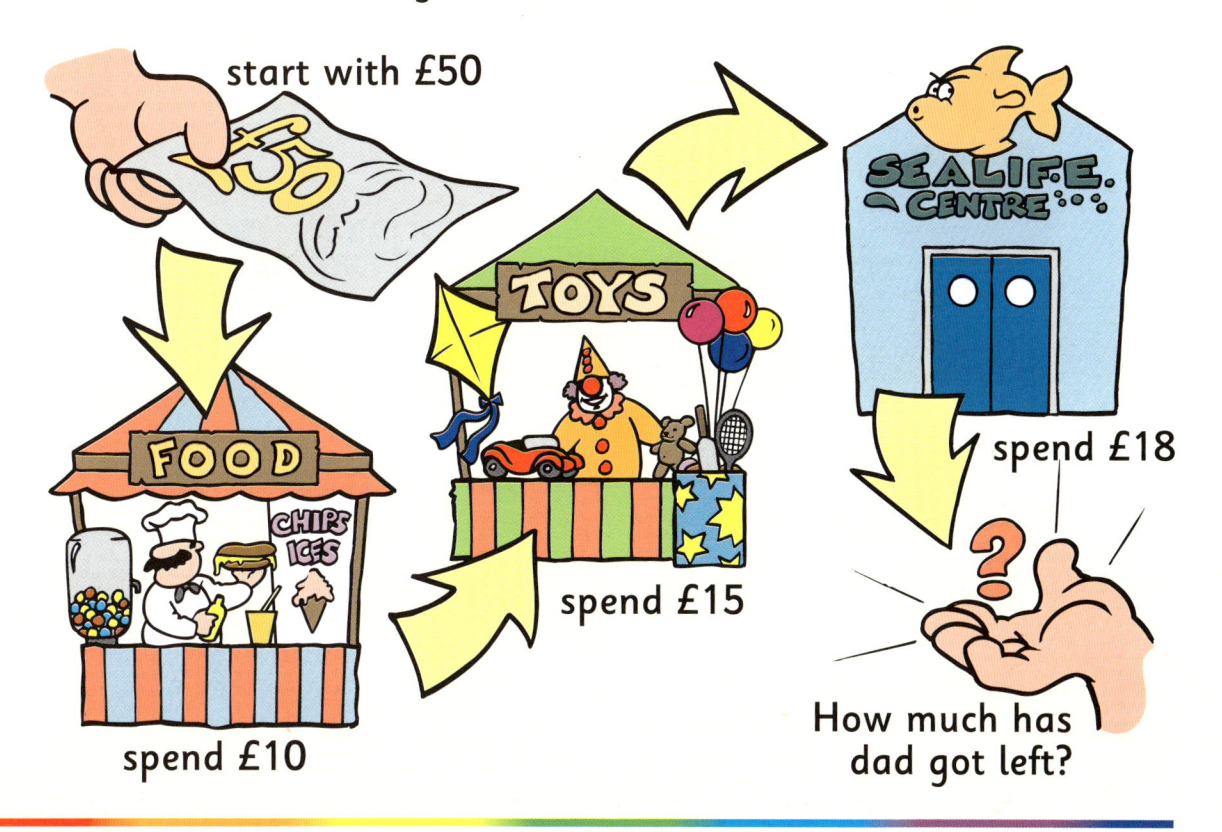

start with £50

spend £10

spend £15

spend £18

How much has dad got left?

---

2 Copy and answer each of these using a mental method.

a 63 − 29
b 54 − 38
c 47 − 19

d 68 − 35
e 57 − 39
f 74 − 32

g 65 − 46
h 92 − 35
i 72 − 35

Challenge

3 a Copy and complete.

£50 − £20 = ■, ■ − £17 = ●, ● − £6 = ▲

b Make up a sum to show how you could start with £70 and finish with £5.

67

Money problems

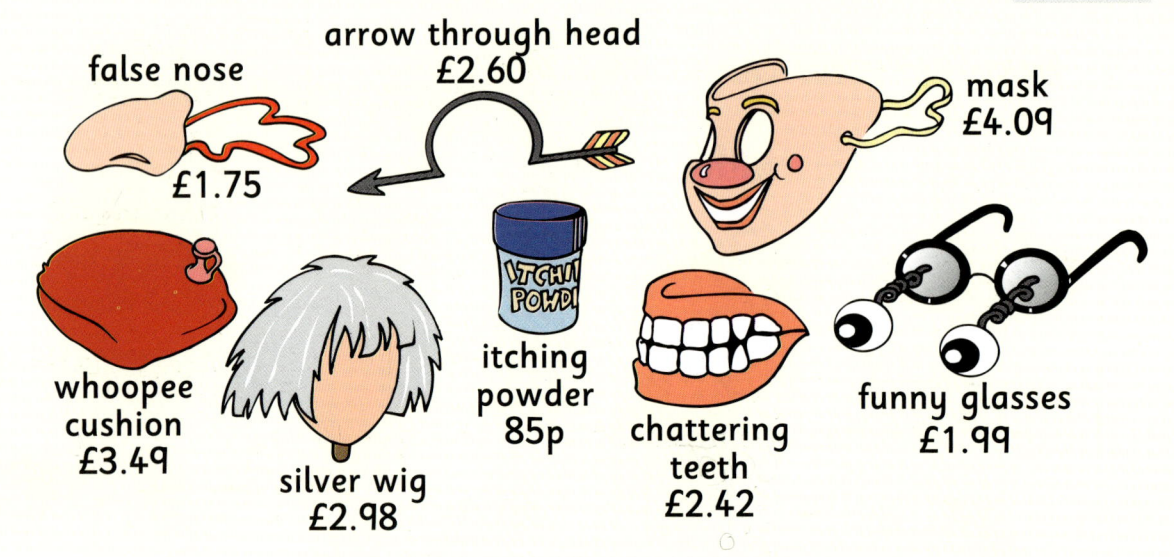

Term 3 Unit 3
Lesson Plans p.56
● Q1, 2

- false nose £1.75
- arrow through head £2.60
- mask £4.09
- whoopee cushion £3.49
- silver wig £2.98
- itching powder 85p
- chattering teeth £2.42
- funny glasses £1.99

1 Write the total price of these items.
Which method will you use?

☆ mask and wig   £7.07 ✓

a arrow and chattering teeth
b whoopee cushion and itching powder
c funny glasses and mask
d false nose and chattering teeth
e silver wig and whoopee cushion

2 What change would you get from £5 for each of these:

☆ whoopee cushion   £1.51 ✓

a mask
b funny glasses
c arrow
d silver wig
e chattering teeth

I can do some of these in my head.

Challenge

3 You have £10 to spend at the joke shop.
Which items would you buy? How much change would you have?

Poster problems

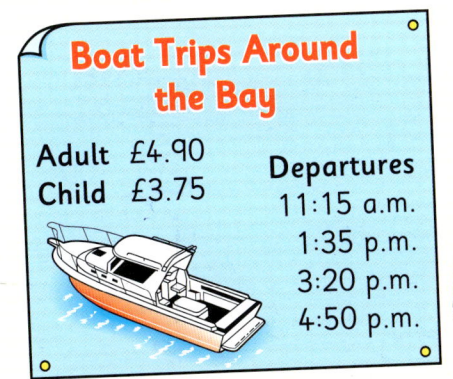

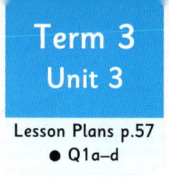

Boat Trips Around the Bay
Adult £4.90
Child £3.75
Departures
11:15 a.m.
1:35 p.m.
3:20 p.m.
4:50 p.m.

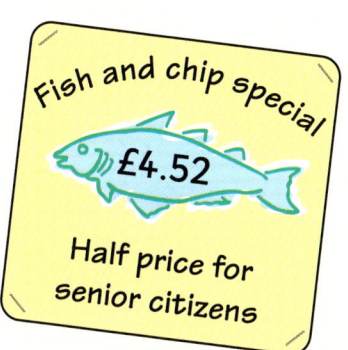

Fish and chip special
£4.52
Half price for senior citizens

Visit the Mini Railway
Top attraction:
17,450 visitors in July
- 945 metres of track
- 4 different engines
- 36 carriages
Adult £1.65   Children 85p

1 Use the information to answer the question.

☆ How much does fish and chips cost for two people?

> £4 × 2 = £8
> 52p × 2 = 104p
> Total = £9.04

a The boat trip takes 55 minutes. When does the 1:35 p.m. trip arrive back?

b How much does fish and chips cost for a senior citizen?

c How much more railway track is needed to make it 1 km long?

d How many carriages are there for each engine?

e Each carriage holds eight people. How many people can fit on each train?

f There were 500 fewer visitors to the railway in August than July. How many visitors in August?

g What is the cost of a boat trip for 1 adult and 2 children?

Challenge

2 What is the total cost for a family of 2 adults and 3 children for:

a A boat trip?

b A ride on the mini railway?

c A fish and chip supper?

Reading scales

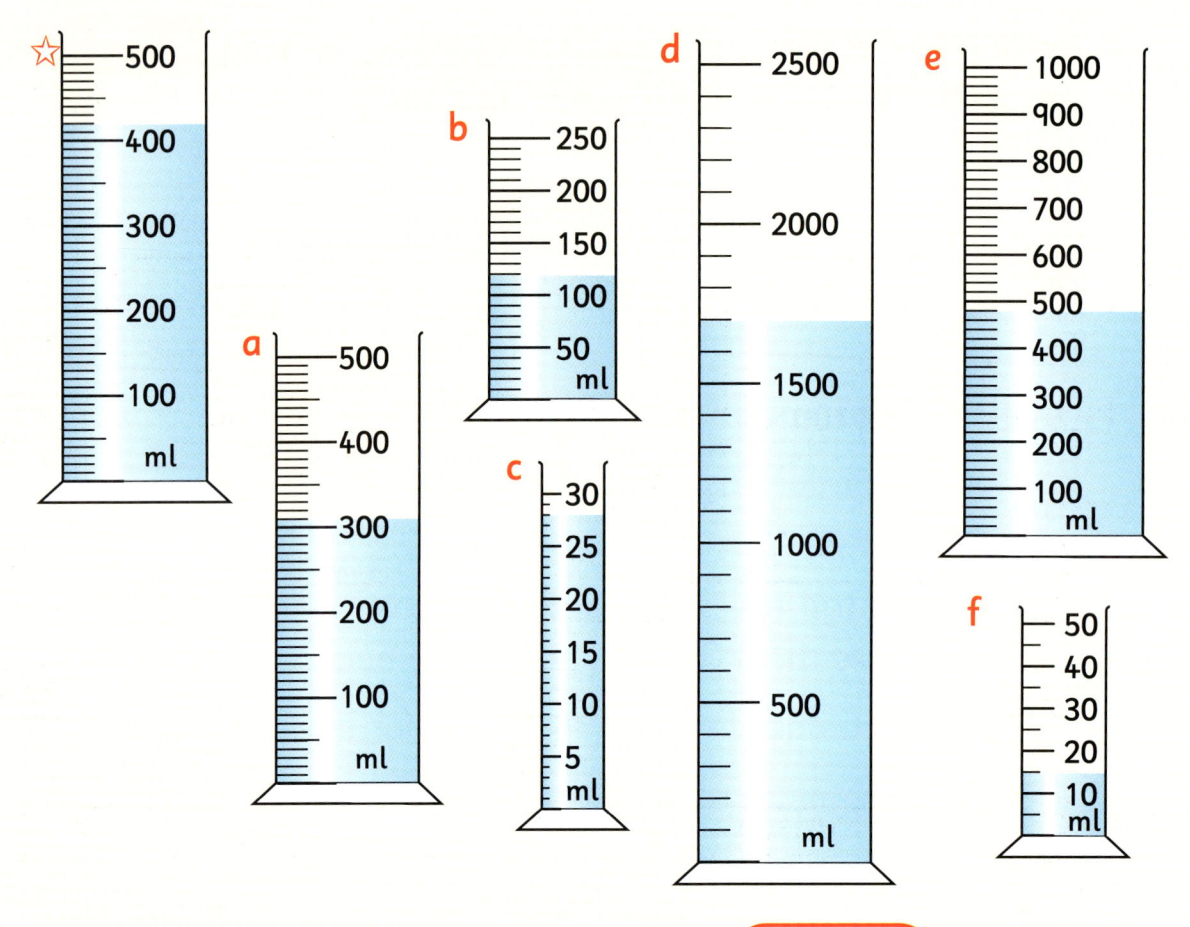

Term 3 Unit 4
Lesson Plans p.58
• Q1–3

1 How much water in each container? ☆ 420 ml

2 How much water is needed to fill each container to the top mark? ☆ 80 ml

3 Write the letters in order of the size of each container, starting with the largest.

Challenge

4 The combined water from four of the containers could be added to **d** without spilling any.
Which four containers? (There is more than one answer.)

Capacity maze

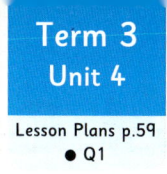

1 Follow the equivalent measures to find your way through the maze of pipes. Write all the measures on your route in two ways.

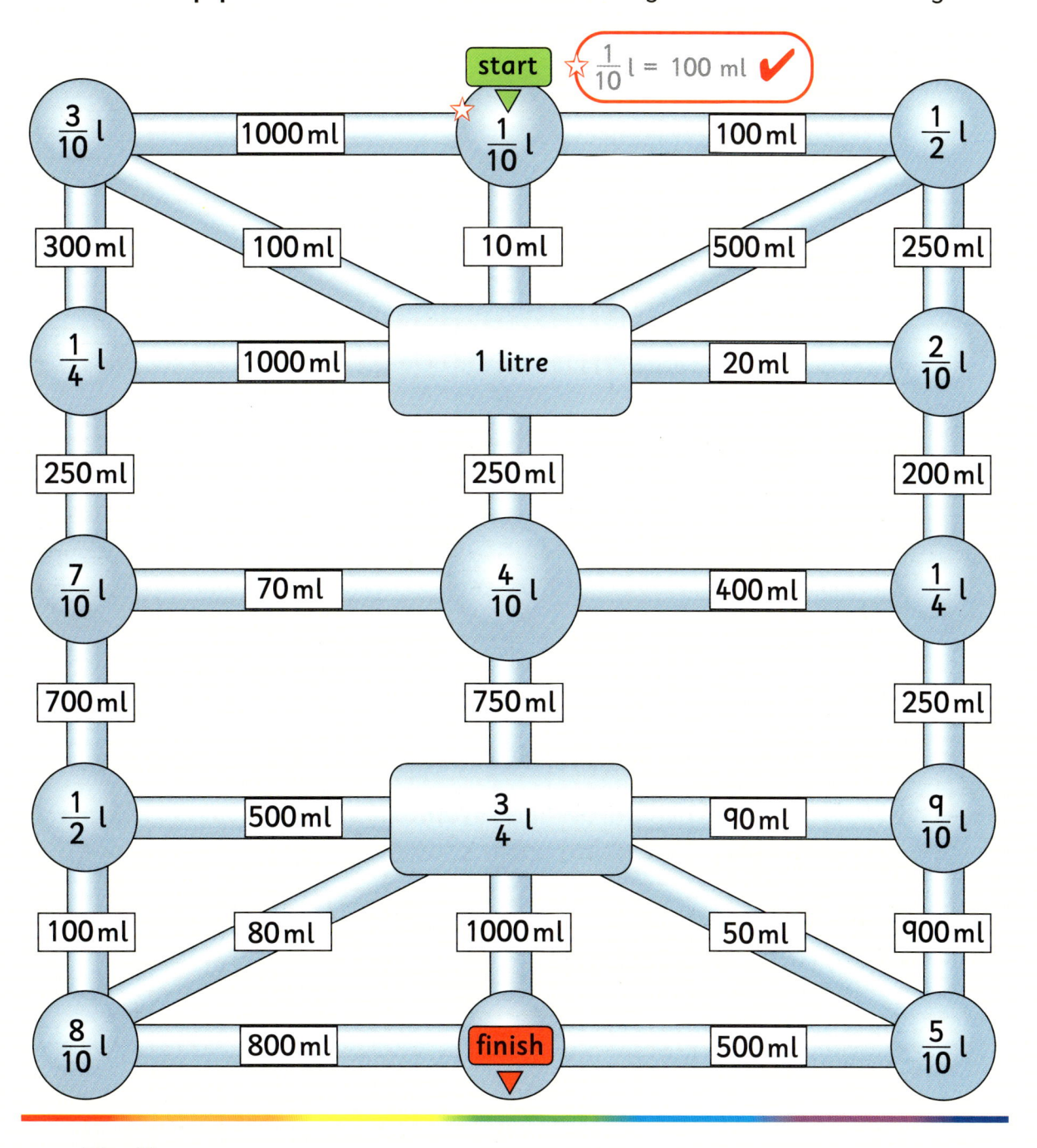

$\frac{1}{10}$ l = 100 ml ✓

start

$\frac{3}{10}$ l	1000 ml	$\frac{1}{10}$ l	100 ml	$\frac{1}{2}$ l
300 ml	100 ml	10 ml	500 ml	250 ml
$\frac{1}{4}$ l	1000 ml	1 litre	20 ml	$\frac{2}{10}$ l
250 ml		250 ml		200 ml
$\frac{7}{10}$ l	70 ml	$\frac{4}{10}$ l	400 ml	$\frac{1}{4}$ l
700 ml		750 ml		250 ml
$\frac{1}{2}$ l	500 ml	$\frac{3}{4}$ l	90 ml	$\frac{9}{10}$ l
100 ml	80 ml	1000 ml	50 ml	900 ml
$\frac{8}{10}$ l	800 ml	finish	500 ml	$\frac{5}{10}$ l

Challenge

2 How much water did you collect on your route?

Capacity problems

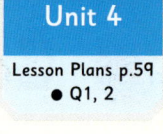

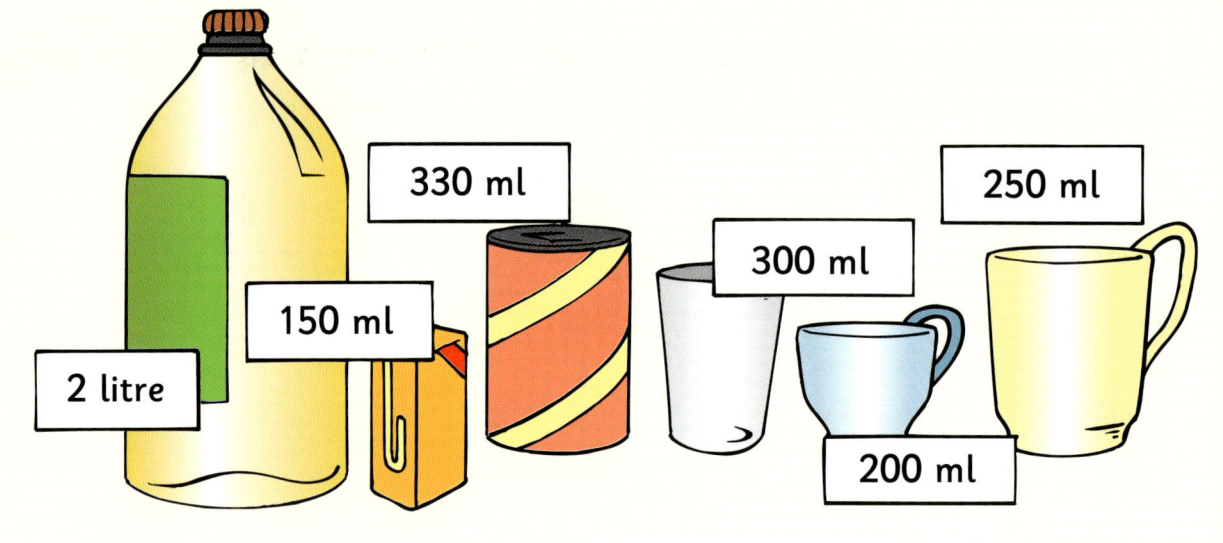

Term 3 Unit 4
Lesson Plans p.59
• Q1, 2

2 litre, **150 ml**, **330 ml**, **300 ml**, **200 ml**, **250 ml**

1 Copy and complete:

a $\frac{1}{2}$ l = ■ ml

b $\frac{1}{4}$ l = ■ ml

c $\frac{3}{4}$ l = ■ ml

d $\frac{1}{10}$ l = ■ ml

2 ☆ How much more does the glass hold than the cup?

a How much more does the can hold than the carton?

b How many mugs can be filled from the bottle?

c How many cups can be filled from the bottle?

> ☆ 300 − 200 = 100
> The glass holds 100 ml more than the cup.

3 a Make a list of everything you had to drink yesterday.

b Approximately how much did you drink?

Challenge

4 Approximately how much do you drink in a week?

How much in a month?

Reflections

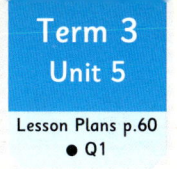

1 Copy this shape and the mirror line on squared paper then draw the shape's reflection.

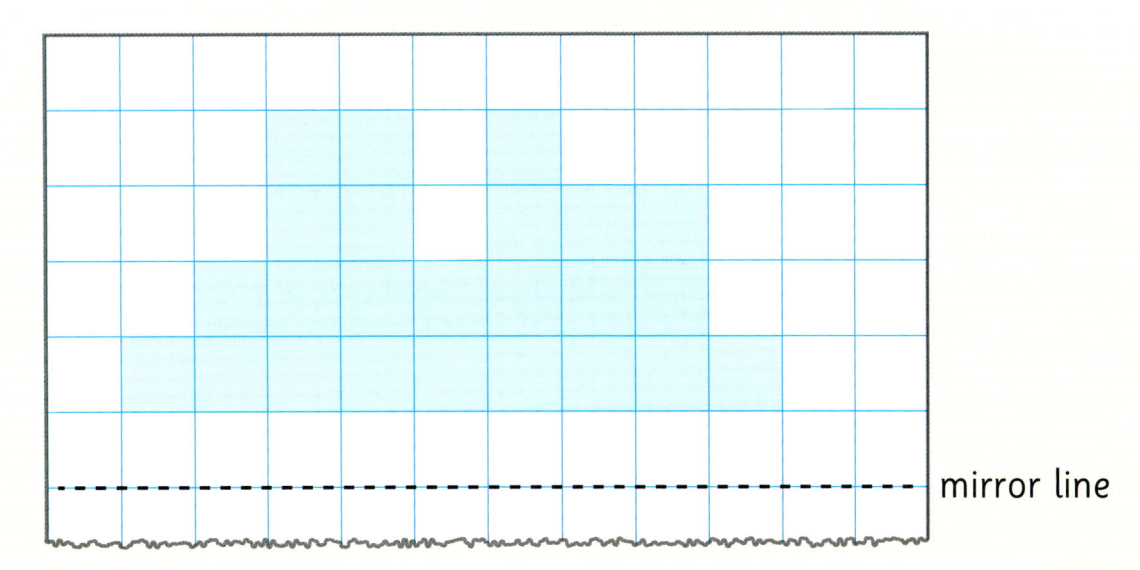

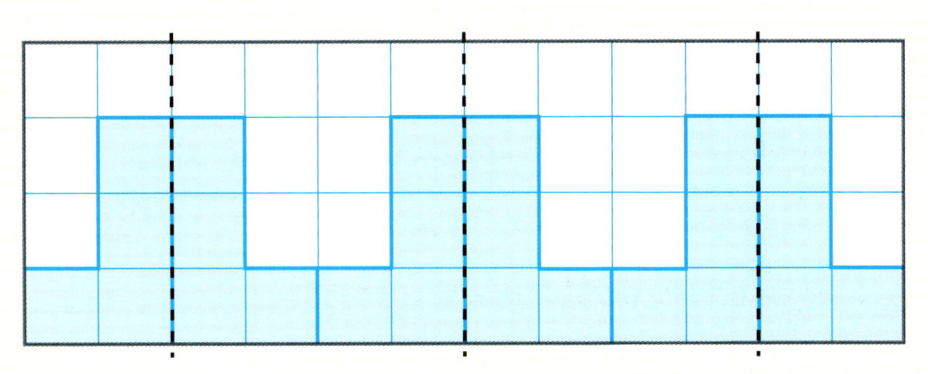

mirror line

2 a This pattern has one shape and its reflection, then it repeats. Continue the pattern in your exercise book.

  b Make up a pattern of your own which reflects a shape then repeats.

Challenge

3 Under your pattern draw its reflection through a horizontal mirror line.

Angles

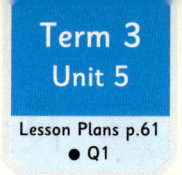

Term 3 Unit 5
Lesson Plans p.61
• Q1

1 Estimate the size of each angle then measure it with a set square.

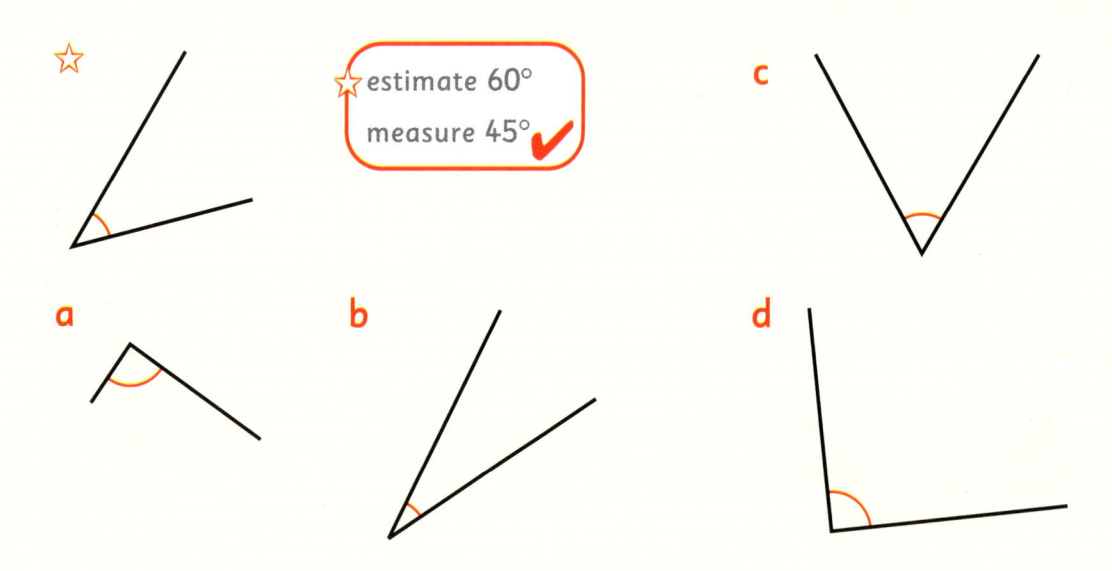

☆ estimate 60°
measure 45° ✓

a

b

c

d

2 Write the angles in order of size, starting with the largest.

Challenge

3 Draw the angles in your exercise book using just a ruler and pencil.
Check with a set square.
How close were you?

Angles on a clock face

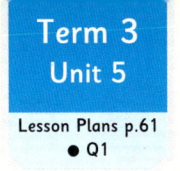

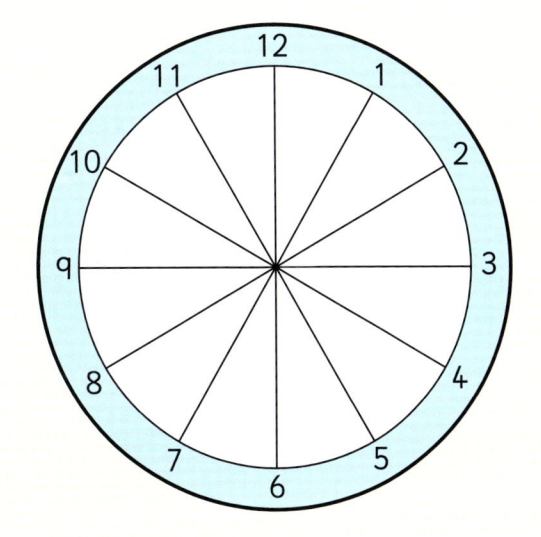

1 What size is the angle between:

☆ 12 and 1? — 30° ✓

a 12 and 2?

b 3 and 6?

c 2 and 4?

d 3 and 9?

e 6 and 10?

f 1 and 6?

g 7 and 8?

h 8 and 12?

2 Estimate the size of each angle.
You might find the clock face helpful.

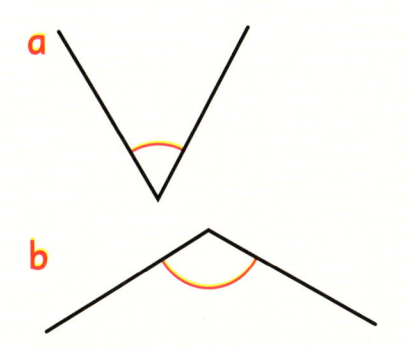

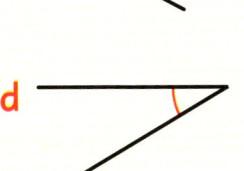

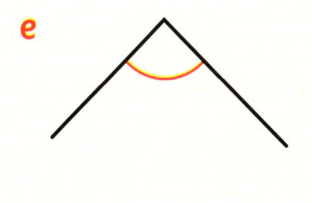

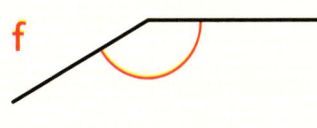

a

b

c

d

e

f

Challenge

3 Fold a piece of paper to try to make an angle of 75°.
Compare with a partner. Is it accurate?
Can you make it more accurate?

Regular shapes

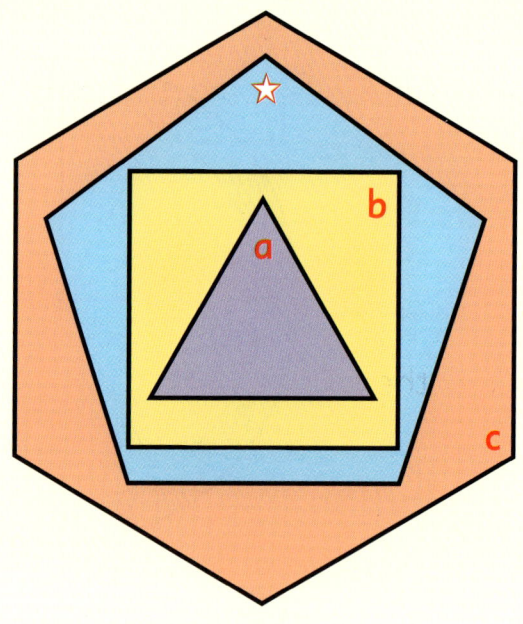

1 Copy the table.

Use an angle measurer to find the angle in the corner of each shape. Complete the table.

shape	a triangle	b square	☆ pentagon	c hexagon
number of sides			5	
angle size			108°	

2 Copy and complete.

In regular shapes, the angles get … as the number of … gets bigger.

Challenge

3 Draw a regular shape with eight sides as carefully as you can.
(Use a template to help if you wish.)

Is the angle bigger or smaller than 120°?
Measure to find out.

Exploring shapes

Term 3 Unit 6
Lesson Plans p.63
● Q1

1 a Draw a square like this on squared paper. Draw the diagonals.

  b Mark all the sides which are equal in the same colour.

  c Mark all the angles which are equal in the same colour.

  d What size are the angles in the middle?

  e Is it the same for all squares? (Check on a square of a different size.)

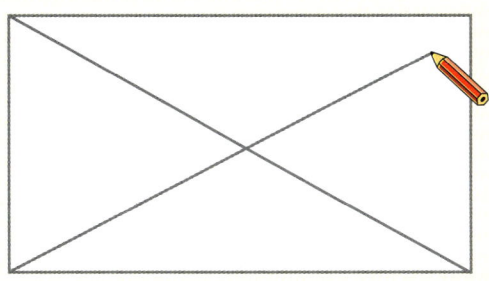

2 a Draw a rectangle like this on squared paper.

  b Mark equal sides and equal angles.

  c Explain how the rectangle is different from the square.

  d Is it the same for all rectangles?

Challenge

3 a Draw around a regular pentagon and draw its diagonals.
  (There are five diagonals altogether.)

  b What do you notice about the shape in the middle?

  c How many triangles can you see?

  d Use colour to show which triangles are the same.

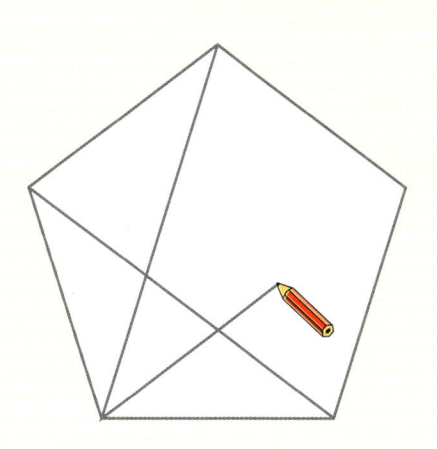

Review: tens, hundreds and thousands

Term 3 Unit 7 Lesson Plans p.63

1 a Round each number to the nearest ten.

☆ 346 ⟶ 350 ✓

☆ 346   678   283   994   597

b Round each number to the nearest hundred.

253   671   436   815   967

2 Copy and complete.

a 43 + ■ = 100
b 72 + ■ = 100
c 2600 + ■ = 3000
d 63 + 40 = ■
e 89 − 35 = ■

f 52 + 34 = ■
g 71 + 29 = ■
h 4000 − 3200 = ■
i 85 + 43 = ■
j 64 + 75 = ■

3 ☆ Salma spends 45p at a shop. How much change does she have from £1.00?

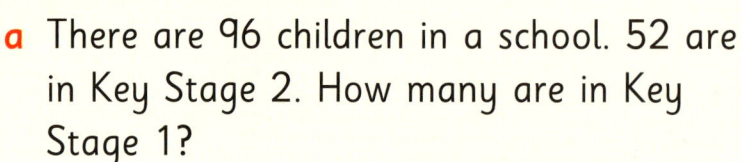

☆ 100 − 45 = 55 ✓
She has 55p change.

a There are 96 children in a school. 52 are in Key Stage 2. How many are in Key Stage 1?

b An aeroplane has travelled 3600 miles. Its whole journey is 4000 miles. How much further does it have to go?

c Rob spends 85p on an ice cream and 52p on a comic. How much does he spend altogether?

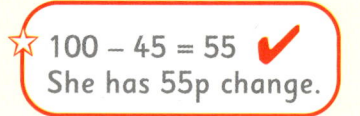

Review: choosing methods

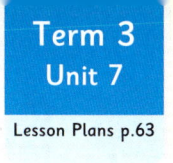

Term 3 Unit 7
Lesson Plans p.63

1 Choose a good way to do each calculation.

☆ 347 + 268

a 325 + 140

b 653 − 284

c 100 − 38

d 36 + 327 + 17 + 125

e 500 + 45

f 758 − 234

g 62 + 73

☆
```
  347
+ 268
-----
  615 ✓
  1 1
```

---

2 Show how you worked out each of these questions.

☆ How much do 3 chocolate bars at 25p each cost altogether?

☆ 25 × 3 = 25 × 2 + 25
      = 50 + 25
      = 75
They cost 75p altogether. ✓

a The perimeter of a square is 40 cm. How long is each side?

b Peter has 374 football cards. Jim has 88 more than Peter. How many cards has Jim?

c Anna has 65p, Max has 78p, Eva has 169p and Mo has 182p. How much do they have altogether? How much more than Max does Mo have?

d One side of an equilateral triangle is 8 cm. How long is the perimeter?

e Dad is 193 cm tall. Steve is 127 cm tall. How much taller is Dad?

Solving a puzzle

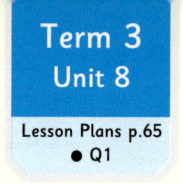

1 **You have 3 red, 3 blue, 5 green and 11 yellow candles.**

Arrange them around a cake in a circle so that no candle is next to another of the same colour.

Draw a diagram to show your answer.

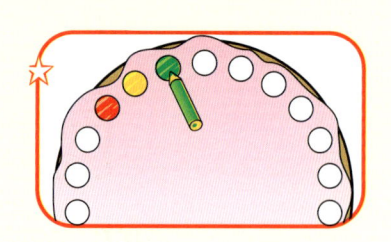

---

2 **How many pencils?**

When Jim counts his pencils in fives he has four left over.

When he counts his pencils in threes he has one left over.

How many pencils does he have?

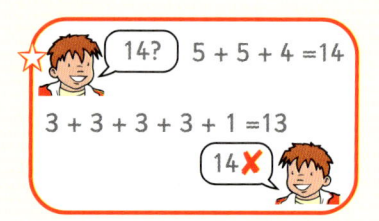

14? 5 + 5 + 4 = 14
3 + 3 + 3 + 3 + 1 = 13
14 ✗

Challenge

3 **Use only 1p and 2p coins.**

Show the different ways you could add them to make every value from 1p to 8p.

How many different combinations are there for each value?
Is there a pattern?
Can you predict how many combinations there will be for 9p, 10p, 20p?

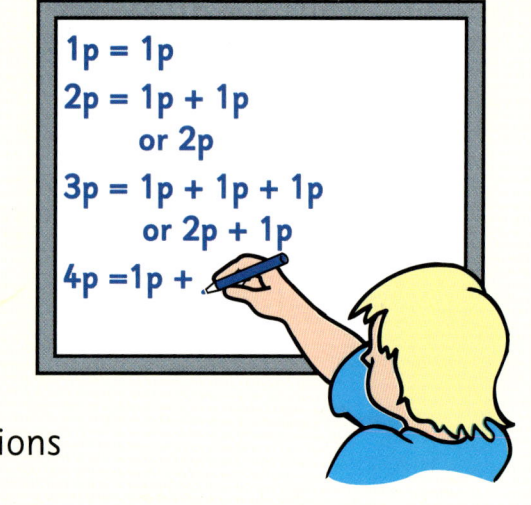

1p = 1p
2p = 1p + 1p
   or 2p
3p = 1p + 1p + 1p
   or 2p + 1p
4p = 1p +

Solving number problems

Term 3 Unit 8
Lesson Plans p.65
• Q1, 2a–c

> 4, 5 and 6 are consecutive numbers
>
> 4 + 5 + 6 = 15
>
> 3 × the middle number (5) = the total (15)

1 Choose which method and number operation to use.

☆ Which three consecutive numbers add to 24?

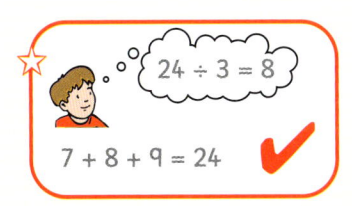

24 ÷ 3 = 8
7 + 8 + 9 = 24 ✓

a Which three consecutive numbers add to 90?

b Which three consecutive <u>even</u> numbers add to 90?

---

2 Each ■ represents a different digit.
Replace each ■ to make the statement true.
Choose from 2, 3, 4 and 7 each time.

☆ 5■ + ■6 = ■9   *53 + 26 = 79* ✓

a 1■ + ■1 = 68
b 8■ − 25 = 6■
c ■ × ■ = ■1
d ■5 + 1■ = 5■
e Find two ways to solve this:
   ■■ ÷ ■ = 8

Challenge

3 Which numbers between 20 and 100 are exactly divisible by 2, 3 and 5?

81

Multiplying TU by U

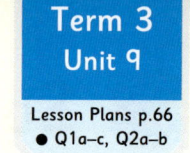

Term 3 Unit 9
Lesson Plans p.66
● Q1a–c, Q2a–b

Show your workings in your exercise book.

1 Split into an addition then multiply to find the answer.

☆ 26 × 4
a 16 × 5
b 51 × 3
c 29 × 4
d 27 × 6
e 43 × 8

☆ 26 × 4 = (20 + 6) × 4
= (20 × 4) + (6 × 4)
= 80 + 24
= 104 ✔

(20 + 6) × 4 has the same value as (20 × 4) + (6 × 4)

2 Choose how to work out these problems.

a 19 players each drink 3 cartons of juice. How many cartons altogether?

b The ground has 5 sections with 28 stewards in each. How many stewards are there?

c 4 fan clubs each bought 47 tickets to the match. How many tickets was that?

d 6 coaches each carried 53 fans to the match. How many fans altogether?

Challenge

3 Find all the products you can make by multiplying each number in turn by each of the others.

2   3   4   5   10

*2 × 3 = 6
2 × 4 = 8
2 × 5 = 10
2 × 10 = 20*

Division with remainders

Term 3 Unit 9
Lesson Plans p.67
• Q1, Q2a–f

Work mentally.

1 Find the remainder.

☆ 16 ÷ 5

☆ 16 ÷ 5 = 3 r 1 ✓

a 19 ÷ 4   **b** 63 ÷ 5   **c** 61 ÷ 3   **d** 74 ÷ 5

e Check your answers: the remainders add to the number of players in a soccer team.

2 Work mentally or write down your workings to find the answers to:

☆ 523 ÷ 100

a 304 ÷ 100   **d** £21 ÷ 4

☆ 523 ÷ 100
500 = 100 × 5
523 − 500 = 23
answer = 5 r 23 ✓

b 799 ÷ 100   **e** £45 ÷ 2

c 54 ÷ 5   **f** £42 ÷ 5

g There are 33 children in Year 4. How many teams of five can be made? How many children will be left over?

h Four tickets cost £37 altogether. How much did one cost?

Challenge

3 Think about dividing by each number from 1 to 10. Which numbers never leave a remainder of 5?

Related facts

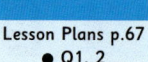

1 List all four related facts.

☆ 5 × 24 = 120

> 5 × 24 = 120
> 24 × 5 = 120
> 120 ÷ 5 = 24
> 120 ÷ 24 = 5 ✓

a 7 × 53 = 371

b 208 ÷ 8 = 26

c 650 ÷ 13 = 50

2 Make a list of the four related facts for each question.

One fact for each set is missing.

To complete a set, write in the missing fact.

> ☆ 100 ÷ 4 = 25
> 100 ÷ 25 = 4
> 4 × 25 = 100
> 25 × 4 = 1

☆ 100 ÷ 4 = 25

8 × 27 = 216

97 × 3 = 291

291 ÷ 3 = 97

39 × 7 = 273

☆ 4 × 25 = 100

291 ÷ 97 = 3

27 × 8 = 216

273 ÷ 7 = 39

216 ÷ 8 = 27

☆ 100 ÷ 25 = 4

7 × 39 = 273

Challenge

3 a Use a fact listed above to solve this problem quickly.

One ticket for the stand costs £27. What is the cost of eight tickets?

b Use another of the facts to make up a problem for your partner.

Solving problems and checking results

Term 3 Unit 10
Lesson Plans p.69
• Q1, Q2a

1 **Check results by approximating.**

☆ 807 adults and 105 children were in the West Stand. How many people altogether?

> 807 + 105 = 912
> 800 + 100
> the answer is approximately 900 ✓

a 798 adults and 89 children were in the North Stand. How many people altogether?

b 97 people each paid £3 for a club badge. How much money altogether?

2 **Explain your solutions in writing.**

☆ Among 30 players, one-sixth are injured. How many are fit?

> Divide 30 by 6, that's 5.
> Then 30 – 5 = 25.
> 25 players are fit. ✓

a I spent half my money. I started with £37. How much did I spend?

b Five people each bought a football at £14. What was the total cost?

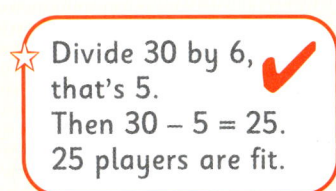

c A footballer signed 20 autographs in one minute. How many could he sign in 8 minutes?

Challenge

3 a Here is the solution. What was the question?
64 – 40 is 24, but this takes away 3 too many, so add back 3 to make the answer 27.

b Make up a problem like this for your partner.

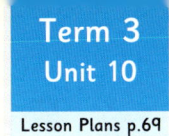

Proportion problems

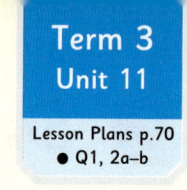

Term 3 Unit 11
Lesson Plans p.70
● Q1, 2a–b

1 Draw necklaces of 12 beads where:

☆ 1 in every 2 beads is striped

a 2 in every 3 beads are coloured

b 1 in every 6 beads is square

c 2 in every 6 beads are striped

d 3 in every 4 beads are green

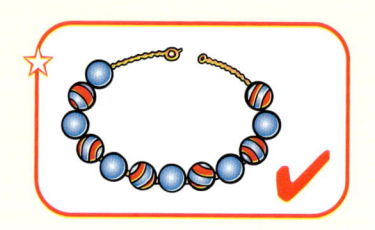

2 For every four cans of cola you buy, you get a plastic toy.

☆ How many toys with 8 cans?

☆ 4 cans = 1 toy
8 cans = 2 toys ✓

a How many toys with 12 cans?

b How many toys with 20 cans?

c How many cans do you need to buy to get four toys?

d How many cans do you need to buy to get seven toys?

Challenge

3 One hundred tiles are needed to cover the floor. One in every five tiles is black, the rest are white. How many black and how many white tiles are needed?

Decimals and fractions

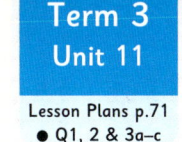

Term 3 Unit 11
Lesson Plans p.71
● Q1, 2 & 3a–c

1 List the decimals and fractions in pairs of the same value.

0.5 $\frac{1}{4}$ 0.3 $\frac{1}{10}$ $\frac{3}{10}$

☆ $\frac{1}{2}$ = 0.5 ✔

$\frac{3}{4}$ 0.25 $\frac{1}{2}$ 0.75   0.1

2 Write each value using decimals.

☆ $3\frac{1}{2}$ kg   ☆ 3.5 kg ✔

a $2\frac{1}{4}$ kg   b $1\frac{3}{4}$ kg   c $4\frac{1}{10}$ kg   d $3\frac{3}{10}$ kg

e $2\frac{5}{10}$ kg

3 Write these lengths in two ways.

☆ $1\frac{1}{4}$ metres   ☆ 1.25 m, 125 cm ✔

a $3\frac{1}{4}$ metres   b $4\frac{1}{2}$ metres   c $7\frac{3}{4}$ metres   d $1\frac{6}{10}$ metres

e $3\frac{9}{10}$ metres

Challenge

4 Forty chocolates were in the box.

How many did each person eat?

Dad: I ate 0.25 of them.
Mum: I ate 0.4 of them.
Steve: I ate 0.3 of them.
Gran: I ate the rest.

87

Term 3 Unit 12
Lesson Plans p.72
• Q1a–e

Relationship between + and –

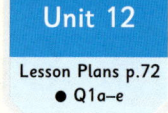

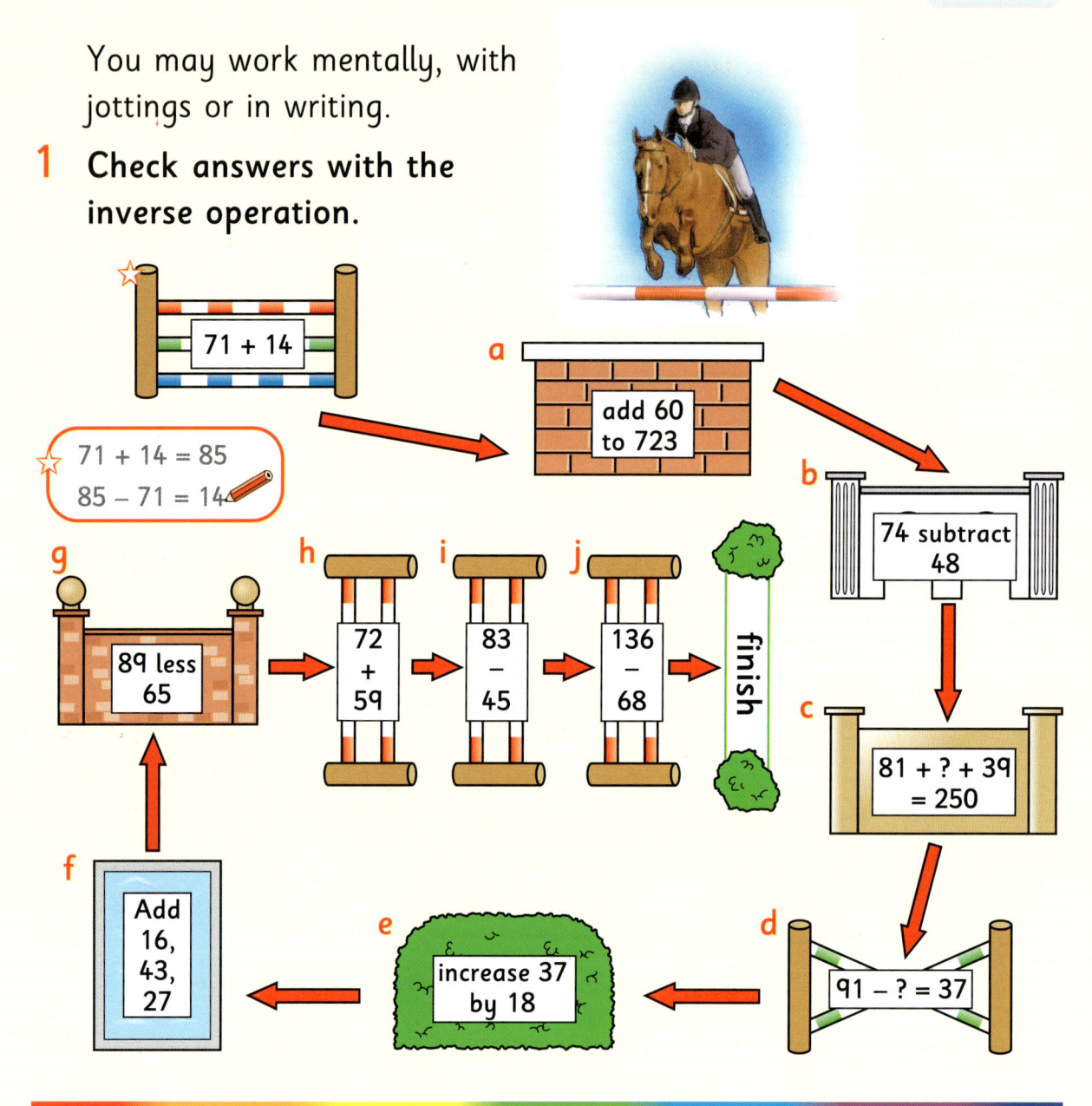

You may work mentally, with jottings or in writing.

1 Check answers with the inverse operation.

71 + 14

71 + 14 = 85
85 – 71 = 14

a add 60 to 723

b 74 subtract 48

c 81 + ? + 39 = 250

d 91 – ? = 37

e increase 37 by 18

f Add 16, 43, 27

g 89 less 65

h 72 + 59

i 83 – 45

j 136 – 68

finish

Challenge

2 Find all the differences you can make using pairs of these numbers:

185   129
214   76   53

Add and subtract mentally

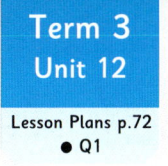

Term 3 Unit 12
Lesson Plans p.72
• Q1

1 Work out each sum mentally.

Look up each answer in the table below to collect a letter.

Use the letters to find out the name of a race written backwards.

Start with the **Y** from the ☆ sum

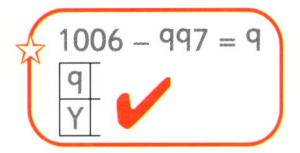

> ☆ 1006 − 997 = 9
>
> 9 / Y ✓

☆ 1006 − 997

- a 2004 − 998
- b 3424 − 9
- c 456 − 8
- d 6000 − 5300
- e 400 + 700
- f 1300 − 500
- g 4643 − 4
- h 600 + 146
- i 78 + 300
- j 1005 − 992
- k 1000 − 700

9	13	300	378	448	700	746	800	1006	1100	3415	4639
Y	R	C	O	N	U	S	C	R	O	T	S

Challenge

2 Use these four digits to make addition and subtraction sums.

Which two of your calculations have answers which add to 800?

| 4 | 0 | 0 | 7 |

Addition and subtraction

Term 3 Unit 12
Lesson Plans p.73
● Q1a–c, Q2a–b

If you need to, use a written method.

$$\begin{array}{r} 934 \\ -868 \end{array} \rightarrow \begin{array}{r} 800 \quad 120 \\ 900 + 130 + 14 \\ -800 + 60 + 8 \\ \hline 60 + 6 \end{array} \quad \begin{array}{r} 8^1 2^1 \\ 9\,3\,4 \\ 8\,6\,8 \\ \hline 6\,6 \end{array}$$

1 Find the difference between the scores of:

☆ Competitors 27 and 23

a Competitors 24 and 26

b Competitors 23 and 25

c Competitors 25 and 28

d Competitors 27 and 25

Points for Event 4	
Competitor 23	868
Competitor 24	780
Competitor 25	736
Competitor 26	714
Competitor 27	934
Competitor 28	648

2 Choose your method of working to find answers to:

☆ 18 + 90 + 26

$$\begin{array}{r} 18 \\ 90 \\ 26 \\ \hline 134 \end{array} \checkmark \quad \text{Answer 134}$$

a 83 + 126 + 97

b 631 − 85

c 806 − 124

d 903 − 167

e Competitor 27 has scored 952 + 948 + 934 + 896 + 988. What is her total score?

Challenge

3 The chart shows how show-jumping points are lost.
Competitor 25 lost 102 points. Investigate the different ways she could have lost the points.

1 time fault loses	2 points
1 fence down loses	30 points
1 refusal loses	40 points

Carroll diagrams

Term 3 Unit 13
Lesson Plans p.74
● Q1

1 Draw a large Carroll diagram like this.

It should almost fill a page in your exercise book.

Quickly sketch and label the shapes in your diagram to complete the display.

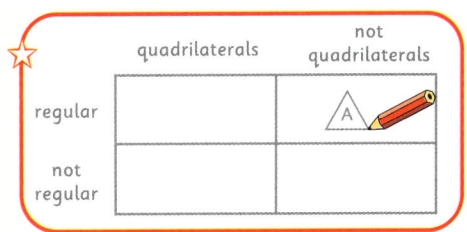

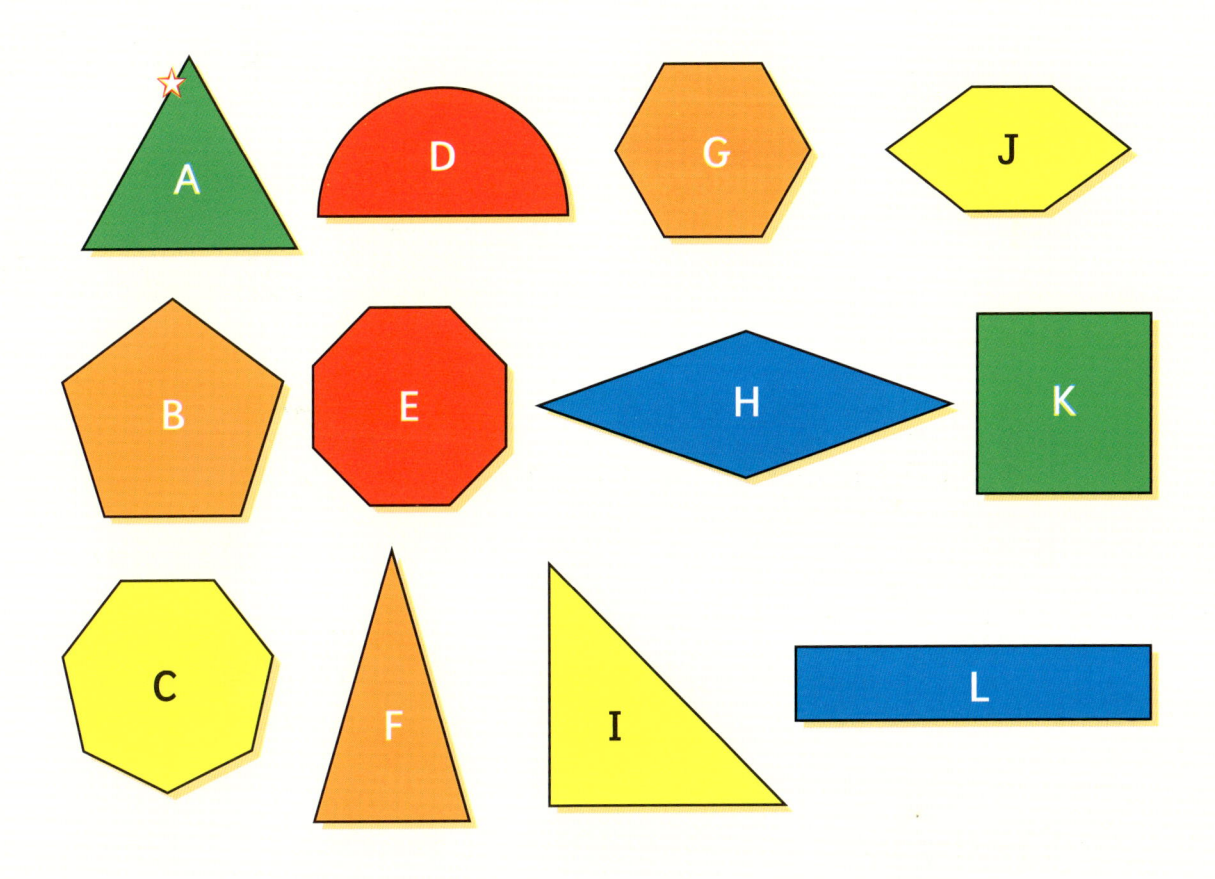

	quadrilaterals	not quadrilaterals
regular		A
not regular		

Challenge

2 a Decide on a different way to sort the shapes. Draw a Carroll diagram. Add labels and complete.

b Hide the labels and ask a partner to guess how the shapes have been sorted.

Venn diagrams

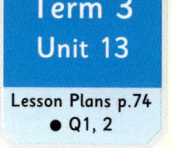

Term 3 Unit 13
Lesson Plans p.74
● Q1, 2

3D shapes

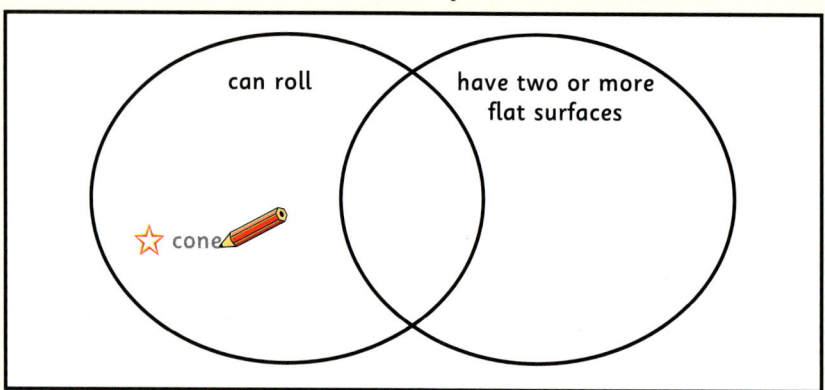

can roll | have two or more flat surfaces

☆ cone

1 Draw this Venn diagram in your exercise book.

Write the names of these 3D shapes in the correct places.

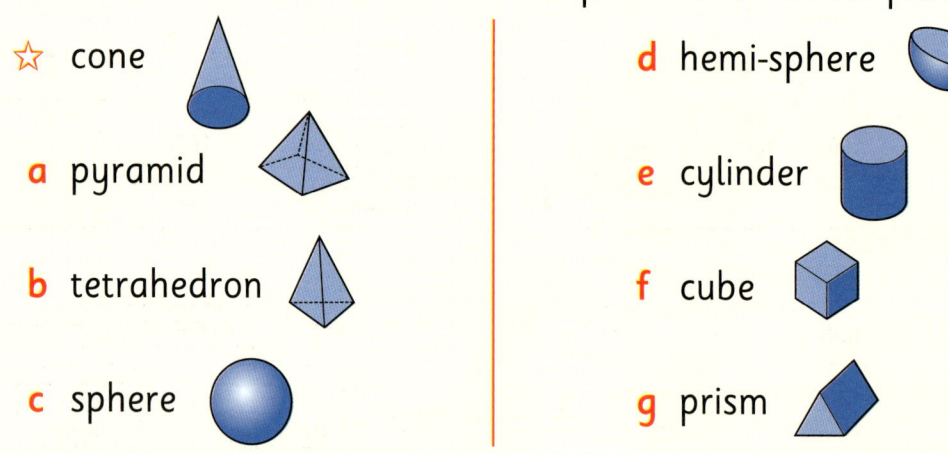

☆ cone

a pyramid

b tetrahedron

c sphere

d hemi-sphere

e cylinder

f cube

g prism

2 Explain how you decided where to place the cylinder.

3 Did you place any shapes outside the rings? Explain why.

Challenge

4 Draw a Venn diagram with the title '3D shapes'.

Make one of the labels say 'has more than two edges'.
Decide what to write on the other label.
Complete the diagram.

Interpreting data in diagrams

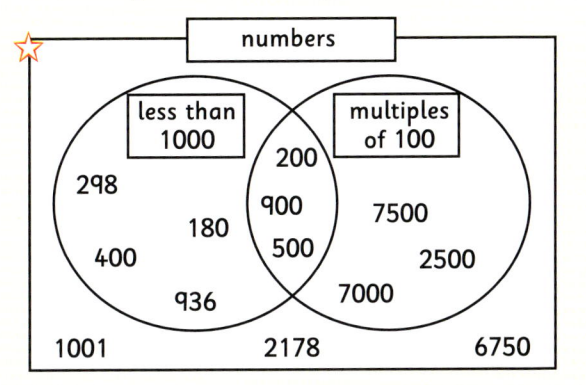

Term 3 Unit 13
Lesson Plans p.75 • Q1

Example diagram (numbers): Venn diagram with "less than 1000" circle containing 298, 180, 400, 936 and "multiples of 100" circle containing 7500, 2500, 7000; intersection contains 200, 900, 500. Outside: 1001, 2178, 6750.

> ★ 400 is in the wrong place. It should be in the intersection because it is also a multiple of 100. ✓

1 One of the numbers is in the wrong place in each diagram.

Record the number and explain where it should be.

a Venn diagram (numbers):
- multiples of 6: 36, 12, 44, 18
- multiples of 10: 50, 70, 600
- intersection: 30, 240, 60
- outside: 11, 25

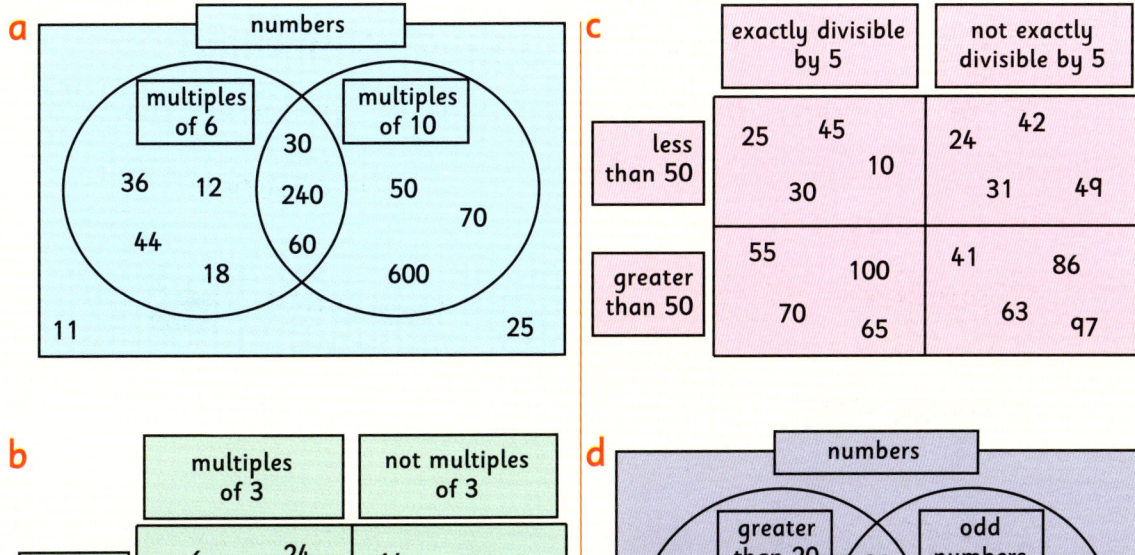

c Carroll diagram:

	exactly divisible by 5	not exactly divisible by 5
less than 50	25, 45, 10, 30	24, 42, 31, 49
greater than 50	55, 100, 70, 65	41, 86, 63, 97

b Carroll diagram:

	multiples of 3	not multiples of 3
even numbers	6, 24, 18, 12	14, 29, 16, 32
odd numbers	33, 15, 21, 39, 27	13, 41, 7, 11

d Venn diagram (numbers):
- greater than 20: 56, 48, 82, 94
- odd numbers: 3, 15, 11
- intersection: 21, 93, 53
- outside: 24, 8, 6

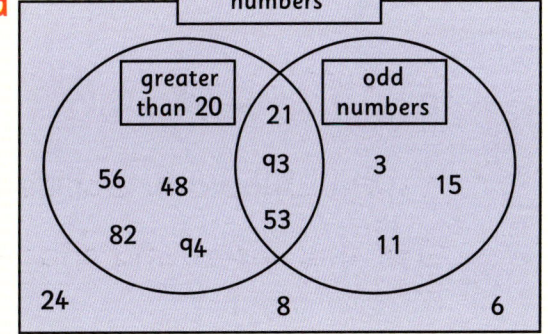

Challenge

2 Which numbers from 45 to 60 are greater than 50 and exactly divisible by 3?

Use a Venn or Carroll diagram to organise and display your answer.

Review: multiplication and division

Term 3 Unit 14
Lesson Plans p.76

Choose how to do each question: mentally, with jottings or in writing.

1 What is the remainder when you divide:

☆ 25 by 3?

> 25 ÷ 3 = 8 r 1
> the remainder is 1 ✓

a 95 by 10?
b 56 by 6?

c 42 by 8?
d 38 by 4?

2 List all four facts related to:

☆ 4 × 9 = 36

> 4 × 9 = 36
> 9 × 4 = 36
> 36 ÷ 4 = 9
> 36 ÷ 9 = 4 ✓

a 26 ÷ 2 = 13
b 300 × 7 = 2100
c 400 ÷ 80 = 5

3 Find answers to:

a double 36
b half of 980
c one eighth of 600
d 257 ÷ 4

4 Round up or down.

☆ One tray holds six jigsaws. How many trays are needed to hold 40 jigsaws?

> 40 ÷ 6 = 6 r 4
> Seven trays are needed. ✓

a How many tickets at £7 can you buy with £38?

The Starbursts in concert Tonight
All tickets £7.00

b Crisps are sold in packs of 6. How many packs are needed to give 32 children a packet of crisps each?

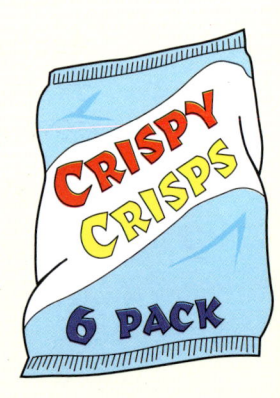

CRISPY CRISPS 6 PACK

Review: addition and subtraction

Choose the number operation and method of calculating.

1 **Find the answers.**

☆ Increase 157 by 84.

$$\begin{array}{r} 157 \\ + 84 \\ \hline 241 \\ {\scriptstyle 1} \end{array}$$ ✓

a Decrease 368 by 173.

b What is the difference between 526 and 183?

c How much altogether is 35p + 17p + 58p + 73p?

---

2 **What is the missing number?**

☆ ▲ + 54 = 164   ☆ 164 − 54 = 110 ✓

a 1500 + ▲ = 2000

b 4003 − ▲ = 7

c ▲ − 6 = 219

---

3 **Find the answers.**

a Here is the money raised at the school fair:

bouncy castle	£37
teas	£32
lucky dip	£28
nearly new	£57

How much was raised altogether?

b Rob sharpened 168 coloured pencils: 39 of them were red, 45 blue and 28 were yellow. The rest were green. How many were green?

Glossary

area
The area of a 2D shape is the amount of surface that it covers. Area is measured in square units such as square centimetres, cm², or square metres, m².

consecutive
Things that are consecutive come one after the other in order. 4, 5 and 6 or 37, 38 and 39 are consecutive numbers because they sit one after the other on the number line.

co-ordinates
Co-ordinates help us to identify a point on a map or grid by using two numbers, such as (3,4). The first number tells us how far across to go and the second number how far up.

data
Data are items of information. The data can be in the form of words, numbers or even pictures.

decimals
Decimals are another way of writing fractions or parts of numbers less than one.
0.5 is a decimal number that means the same as $\frac{1}{2}$.

divisible by
If a number is divisible by another number it can be divided exactly with no remainder. Ten is divisible by two because two divides exactly into ten. Ten is not divisible by three because the division is not exact:
10 ÷ 3 = 3 r 1

equilateral triangle
An equilateral triangle has three equal sides and three equal angles. It is a regular shape.

heptagon
A heptagon is a 2D shape with seven straight sides and seven vertices (corners).

inverse operation
Inverse means opposite so the inverse of a number operation is the opposite operation. Addition and subtraction are inverse operations and so are multiplication and division.

irregular polygon
An irregular polygon has sides of different lengths and angles of different sizes.

isosceles triangle
An isosceles triangle has two equal sides and two equal angles.

net
A net is a shape drawn on paper or card that can be cut out and folded to make a 3D shape.

perimeter
The perimeter of a 2D shape is the distance all the way round the outside. It is measured as a length in mm, cm or m.

polygon
A polygon is a 2D shape with any number of straight-sides. Triangles, quadrilaterals, pentagons and hexagons are all different types of polygon

quotient
A quotient is an answer to a division sum. The quotient of 12 and 3 is 4. The quotient of 17 and 5 is 3 r 2.

regular polygon
A regular polygon has all sides of equal length and all angles of equal size.

tetrahedron
A tetrahedron is a 3D shape made up of four triangular faces. It is sometimes called a triangular-based pyramid.